MIXED COMPANY

Dedicated to Buddy Pouyatt

MIXED COMPANY:
THREE EARLY JAMAICAN PLAYS

Edited by Yvonne Brewster

Maskarade **by Sylvia Wynter**

Bedward **by Louis Marriott**

The Creatures **by Cicely Waite-Smith**

OBERON BOOKS
LONDON

WWW.OBERONBOOKS.COM

This collection first published in 2012 by Oberon Books Ltd
521 Caledonian Road, London N7 9RH
Tel: +44 (0) 20 7607 3637 / Fax: +44 (0) 20 7607 3629
e-mail: info@oberonbooks.com
www.oberonbooks.com

PB ISBN: 978-1-84943-216-0
EPUB ISBN: 978-1-84943-634-2

Cover image: Costume design by Ellen Cairns for Pitchie Patchie
in Talawa Theatre Company's 1993 production of *Maskarade*
directed by Yvonne Brewster.

Visit www.oberonbooks.com to read more about all our books
and to buy them. You will also find features, author interviews and
news of any author events, and you can sign up for e-newsletters
so that you're always first to hear about our new releases.

Contents

Introduction   7
Yvonne Brewster

Introduction to *Maskarade*   20
Sylvia Wynter and Yvonne Brewster

Maskarade: A 'Jonkunnu' Musical Play   23
Sylvia Wynter

Introduction to *Bedward*   137
Louis Marriott

Bedward: A Play in Two Acts   140
Louis Marriott

Melodic lines for songs by Noel Dexter   204

Introduction to *The Creatures*   211
Honor Ford-Smith

The Creatures   223
Cicely Waite-Smith

Notes on Contributors   254

Acknowledgements   256

Introduction

Yvonne Brewster

In 1935 Marcus Garvey migrated to London in the final chapter of his mission to emancipate the minds of black people everywhere. It was a time when native Jamaicans at home and abroad started dreaming of freedom from the yoke of British colonialism.

The Great Depression between the two world wars had deepened the socio-economic misery that the masses still suffered a hundred years after the abolition of slavery. Trade unions emerged. Industrial disputes sometimes degenerated into riots. Plans were made to establish a political movement designed to end an electoral franchise based on wealth, to extend the vote to all adult Jamaicans, and to achieve Jamaican self-government.

In Britain, in 1938, an article in *The Daily Telegraph* read *inter alia*: 'A great deal is amiss with the economic and social conditions in Jamaica. The truth is that we are now reaping the harvest of a country's neglect. The time has come when it is incumbent upon Britain to apply herself earnestly to the task of redressing the more fundamental causes of West Indian discontent.'

That was a comparatively mild rebuke. Former British Prime Minister David Lloyd George, credited as the architect of the welfare state, had dubbed Jamaica and other British Caribbean colonies the 'slums of the Empire' and British commentators repeatedly contrasted the appalling socio-economic conditions of the Caribbean colonies with the enormous wealth that had accumulated in Britain through the proceeds of West Indian slavery and colonialism.

After a series of significant outbreaks of violence in Jamaica in mid-1938, in November of that year, a large West India Royal Commission from Britain toured Jamaica and other colonies for a close examination of social and economic conditions but also viewed the political landscape.

The sympathetic demeanour of the Royal Commission, under the leadership of Lord Moyne, was encouraging, as was its report. The Colonial Office soon signalled its intent to move Jamaica forward, but the advancement schedule was bedevilled by the outbreak of the Second World War and the posting in Jamaica of a tough new Governor, Sir Arthur Richards, who was accused of conveniently using the war regulations to incarcerate and thus neutralise the most radical and progressive leaders of the new political movement which had been launched in September 1938, highlighting its demand for universal adult suffrage and constitutional progress toward self-government.

Still, in late 1944, a new constitution took effect, inaugurating a governance structure described as 'semi-representative'. The former unicameral Legislative Council, which included members elected under a severely limited franchise sharing law-making responsibility with ex-officio members and gubernatorial appointees, was then transformed into a totally nominated Upper House of a bicameral legislature. The lower chamber was the new House of Representatives comprising 32 members elected in single-member constituencies under universal adult suffrage.

An Executive Council was culled from this hybrid legislature, but real power remained in the hands of the appointees and the Governor held the highest trump. He could take exclusive control of any matter simply by declaring it one of 'paramount importance'. The first step towards an independence-bound federation of the British Caribbean colonies was taken when the British Secretary of State for the Colonies, Arthur Creech Jones, joined delegates from West Indian countries in a 'Closer Association' Conference in Montego Bay, Jamaica.[1]

The first Jamaican to be Chief Minister whilst Jamaica was still a Colony was Alexander Bustamante who held the post for two years (1953-1955) followed by his cousin Norman Manley (1955-1962). Jamaica became a member of the short-lived Federation of the West Indies 1958-1962. Full independence from the United Kingdom was achieved on the 6th August 1962.

The practice of theatre in Jamaica is nothing new. The first formal theatre was built as long ago as 1750. In fact there have existed no fewer than three large theatres in Kingston on the same site in downtown Kingston. The Ward Theatre designed by the Jamaican Rudolph Henriques, which replaced the second

---

1   Excerpt from Louis Marriott's unpublished journals.

Theatre Royal on the site after the 1907 earthquake had done its worst, was a gift to the city of Kingston from its then Custos Colonel C.J. Ward in 1912. With a capacity of just over 900 in its three layers of seating (Parquet, Dress Circle and the Gods), the Ward was recognised as a national Monument in 2000[2] as the only surviving example of a Victorian cum Edwardian style theatre in Jamaica and the rest of the English-speaking Caribbean.

It may be of interest to note here the Ward, with the exception of one or two details, is exceedingly similar to the Theatre Royal in London's Stratford East (1844) designed by James George Buckle, with one important distinction: it is virtually twice the size of the London theatre which seats only 460 people on its three layers.

For nearly two centuries (1750-1941) these buildings provided a comfortable, even luxurious, Kingston venue for performances of plays and other entertainments. At first touring companies from the United Kingdom paid regular visits, the performances in these Theatre Royals were intended exclusively for those in high places (slave owners and the merchant classes, not slaves and the working classes) except, ironically, high up in the 'Gods' where a certain amount of segregated seating was permitted until riots in 1815 put an end to that. In the early nineteen hundreds theatre companies from the United States of America considered a tour to Kingston as something to aim for. By the third and fourth decades of the twentieth century Jamaicans began to take part in this activity, culminating in the development of the annual Pantomime in around 1941, after which the flavour, text, and increasingly the subject matter represented more local concerns and flavour.

The simmering hankering after the good old days of the foreign imports continued. George Bernard Shaw, whilst on a visit to Jamaica in 1911, sought to advise the locals on the wisdom of encouraging local writing and acting and warned that the consequence of continuing to regard foreign work in such a favourable light would be a Jamaican theatre which was vulgar and degraded.

---

2   Sadly, the Ward Theatre is now (December 2011) in urgent need of repair and refurbishment.

In certain quarters some still hankered after the good old days but the wealth of talent and imagination always readily available created a vibrant sustainable culture of producing locally written plays. The Caribbean Thespians, the Little Theatre Movement and The University Players, amateur in name but professional in nature, are landmark local organisations which made invaluable contributions to the development of a local brand of writing for, acting in and direction of Jamaican theatre in the late Forties and the Fifties. Many of those who actively participated in these organisations in this burgeoning locally significant theatre scene have become household names in the arts of the Caribbean. They include Wycliffe Bennett, Slade Hopkinson, Mona Chin (Hammond), Derek Walcott, Ronnie Harrison, Noel Vaz, Easton Lee, Leonie Forbes, Trevor Rhone, Charles Hyatt and Louis Marriott to name but a few.

On August 6th 2012 Jamaica celebrates the 50th anniversary of Independence. *Mixed Company* is a collection of three of the finest early Jamaica theatrical works, written for the most part before the dawn of Independence.

Written in 1954 (*The Creatures* by Cicely Waite-Smith), 1960 (*Bedward* by Louis Marriott) and 1970 (*Maskarade* by Sylvia Wynter), the plays are examples of works conceived with a Jamaican audience in mind, a Jamaican audience conscious of the melting pot in which it lived. Each offers a unique perspective on the spirit of a people who held on to traditional beliefs and customs in the face of colonial opprobrium as the populace struggled to gain its political, social and cultural independence.

There exist some, possibly tenuous, links between the three playwrights. In the case of Alexander Bedward, Waite-Smith writes in her autobiography of her experience in Kingston of the 1930s: 'In the middle of the night...I was startled awake by the sound of tramping feet accompanied by a high strong wail of singing. The sounds advanced and swelled. It was like a singing army on the march, fast and urgent as if the soldiers expected the order to break into a run. Tramp, tramp hallelujah, the energetic statement of many feet and voices.

We shall know (we shall know echoed the chorus)
As we are known (as we are known)
Never more (never more)
To walk alone (to walk alone)
In the purple of the morning
Of that bright and happy day…

"What is it? Who are they? Where are they going?"

"Up to Hope River to be baptised", F told me. "Look out the window. You'll see them."

I ran to the window. All dressed in pure white they were, some with turbans of white and holding high their coloured banners lit by the torches carried by their leaders.

"To be baptised in the cold river like this at one in the morning?"

"Just as you see them, fully clothed. And they'll be back at dawn still singing their heads off."

The night pulsed with their ardour. The trees and telephone poles moved, the road slid away under them like a snake, flowers and shrubs writhed, a window pane across the street flashed like lightning. We shall know, as we are known…'.

Louis Marriott in his introduction to *Bedward* celebrates the life-changing effect his discovery of the Bedward story some two decades later in the 1950s, he having had so little local history taught at his Secondary school. In the *Sunday Gleaner* of March 12th 1972 Sylvia Wynter published an important article which challenged the view of Marcus Garvey as a dreamer and Alexander Bedward as a lunatic. What drove both men she believed was 'the basic revolt of men against their being made merchandise.'

There are other areas social, geographical, historical and religious which these plays have in common. They are not urban, nor are they necessarily of the deep countryside, straddling as they all do, the semi-urban fringes of society. This is important as it was in these fringe environments that cultural tradition, 'roots', stood a better chance of robust survival. Apart from being good scripts for acting and producing, with the many vibrant characters which abound, they all have rebellion at heart:

rebellion in many forms and guises but sharing a common desired outcome of self-determination. They are all written with care to reproduce the rhythms and cadences of Jamaican speech of the time. The Jamaican relationship to rivers and their healing and dangerous qualities, has existed for as long as recorded time. Rivers and hills are of seminal importance in the plays as places of healing, support and mystery: In *Bedward* the Hope River plays a fundamental part in the success of his Ministry; it was in the Hope River he healed the sick. In *The Creatures* the river is the centrifugal force here. The hills in *Maskarade* are the magnetic force. Not surprising, set as they are in a country whose original Arawak name Xaymaca means 'land of wood and water'.

Traditional beliefs, practices and customs are common themes which permeate the plays. Although they have all been mistaken at one time or another as being plays for schools only, they all have very dark underbellies which encompass suicide, a double murder, and improper committal to a mental asylum of a prophet who threatened the status quo, all of which should concern adults too. The quality of writing, the stylistic sophistication, the broad imaginative canvasses they occupy need no apology.

In *Maskarade* the very act of keeping the age-old tradition brought from Africa of enacting the annual Jonkunnu festival is unlawful. The play begins with the festival troupe travelling to the hills above Kingston in search of refuge from persecution. Another kind of rebellion beats at the heart of *Maskarade*: the rebellion of the betrayed older lover in the face of her rejection for a newer model. This sub-plot (although it is too essential in the scheme of things to call it thus) brings the day to day existence into blinding focus. In *Maskarade* the hills are the source of protection and the constant background for the narrators of the piece. This is important to the proper understanding of the text and the playwright in her notes on the setting of the piece suggests 'opposition of the Blue Mountains, the plains and the sea' should be carefully configured.

The tradition of 'playing Jonkunnu' is deep-seated in the Jamaican people. In modern times the practice is often frowned upon as an embarrassment, dismissed as 'old-time rubbish' by sections of the middle classes, simply ignored or, worse fate of all, consigned to the bin marked tourist attraction. Perhaps this is a result of a lack of an awareness, or a culture which is too geared towards tomorrow. The manifestation of Jonkunnu in the culture of Jamaica is too fundamental and too deeply rooted in African and European tradition and belief to ever be truly disregarded because of the continuing fascination with the ritual: the Jonkunnu play *Koo Koo, or Actor Boy* by Sam Hilary, the Jamaican playwright, is well remembered as a fine piece of theatre seen at the Barn Theatre in 1967, and the new (2011) journal of the Edna Manley College is called 'Jonkunnu'. Sylvia Wynter's play *Maskarade* holds a timely, entertaining, sometimes frightening call to cultural arms.

Bedward, set principally in August Town, above Papine, near to the Hope River where town meets country, tells the story of a Jamaican they sometimes called a prophet. Alexander Bedward (1840?1846?, 1848?[3]-1930) was a rebel; the victim of massive prejudice from the ruling classes which manifested itself in persecution and which became more intense the more he succeeded in his mission to provide a mode of worship to which the black man could relate.

Contrary to sensational newspaper reportage of the time, his Jamaica Native Baptist Free Church, founded in 1888, enjoyed phenomenal success with him at the helm as its charismatic faith healer and Bishop. His followers included numerous foreigners – mainly Panamanians, Cubans, Costa Ricans and Americans who journeyed to August Town to be healed. The size of his following, estimated at thirty thousand, especially when viewed in the context of the lack of mass communication at that time, was impressive.

In *Bedward* the battle lines are clearly drawn. Bishop Alexander Bedward was a pioneer advocate of black emancipation, a generation before Marcus Garvey. Alongside his call for social justice in Jamaica, his ministry placed categorical demands for the right to worship according to one's beliefs and cultural background. His rhetoric included the call to arms... 'We are going to have a great battle in this Church against the forces of evil...[a] battle against those who are against the poor that we

3   Opinions vary on the year of Alexander Bedward's birth. No birth certificate exists.

must stand for.' He believed this was necessary as the rich could 'stand for themselves': 'The Pope of Rome and the Archbishop of Canterbury take good care of them'[4].

Cicely Waite-Smith (Howland) wrote *The Creatures* in 1954. Canadian born, English educated, French trained in theatre, she married a Jamaican businessman, and clearly appreciated the culture of her new Jamaican compatriots. She is known to have identified with the struggle for Universal Adult Suffrage towards the goal of Independence. This delicate play, the earliest and probably the most rural of the trio, finds its home on the banks of a river a short bus ride away from the metropolis. It exhibits great sensitivity for the traditions, language and political aspirations of the people of Jamaica at that time. Written in gentle but telling style with dialogue which maintains for the most part a standard English format but which has a subtle, distinctive Jamaican identity when spoken: e.g. 'Miss Mae Lord me God the man nearly killed me, my head spinning round – my knees are giving away – '. While other playwrights were perhaps more overtly interested in the political or the religious, Waite-Smith carved out a space which allowed for the co-existence and interplay of birds, reptiles and natural phenomena with the everyday lives, times, beliefs and aspirations of the Jamaican. The river is the source of wisdom, peace, community gatherings and, perhaps more importantly for purposes of the play, the home of River Mumma, and whose deep waters accommodate the tragedy.

The traditional folkloric character River Mumma, is evoked with such power in *The Creatures* that the pull of the African ancestors and of vibrant handed-down mythology is all the more irresistible. She is described as a 'handsome and seductive woman, wearing a dark greenish gown'. The Fisherman calls her simply Woman. He is on intimate speaking terms with her and Yellowlegs and Lizard. This play has sometimes been regarded as exclusively children's literature because of the important part the bird of passage (Yellowlegs) and Lizard[5] play, but to do so is

---

4   *Bedward*: Act One, Scene 3.

5   The Lizard may very well be the serpent. Yellowlegs might very well be the Yellow Bird of the well-known song. However, birds do have a particular significance in Jamaican culture. In some forms of local belief systems the egg is sacred. In the ceremony held nine nights after death, a large bread in the shape

to ignore the very dark social anger, the almost hopelessness of the peasant who has to seek fortune in the city, leaving behind the more important things in life and being coarsened in the process. This runs like the river beneath the play.[6] It is not surprising that *The Creatures* was reportedly a favourite with Jamaican cultural/political icons Edna Manley,[7] sculptor wife of Norman Manley,[8] and Rex Nettleford[9].

The Creatures is a play in One Act. In spite or perhaps because of its succinctness, in its brevity it paints a clear picture of a small enclave of simple people about to lose its innocence, as seen through the eyes of a henpecked old fisherman who continues to struggle to gain his independence from his insensitive wife. His rebellion is small, personal and alive.

In this, the 50th year of Jamaica's Independence when the theatre scene is so alive and dynamic and immediate, perhaps it is no bad thing to pause for a while and appreciate some of the first plays written solely with a Jamaican audience in mind.

Derek Walcott once suggested that to be universal one must first be specific. I think these plays qualify.

---

of a bird dominates the setting. This is meant to represent the journey the spirit will have to undertake. It must fly.

6 Sylvia Wynter wrote in her wide-ranging paper: 'Jonkunnu in Jamaica: Towards the interpretation of folk dance as a cultural process': '*Jamaica too had its water-dance to the water spirit, or river goddess. This spirit known as "Ribba Mumma" was supposed to: "Inhabit every fountainhead of an inexhaustible and considerable stream of water in Jamaica." The slaves, in times of drought, used to persuade their master to sacrifice an ox at the fountainhead of the water turning the mill. The water spirit was supposed to materialize like a mermaid at noon, combing her long black hair…*'.

7 It was in the 1956 edition of Edna Manley's Literary Magazine *Focus* produced by the Extra Mural Department of the University College of the West Indies, that I first came upon *The Creatures* (Ed.).

8 The 2nd Prime Minister of Independent Jamaica.

9 Founder and Artistic Director of the National Dance Theatre of Jamaica and Trade Union Academic.

MASKARADE

A 'JONKUNNU' MUSICAL PLAY

BY SYLVIA WYNTER

Cast in order of appearance:

LOVEY	Traditional Storyteller
BOY	His apprentice, 12 years old
DRIVER	Coachman to the Mayor of Kingston
	plays King
BRIANSY	A Tailor plays Pitchie Patchie
DEAF MUTE	Assistant to Brainsy plays Houseboat
MAUD	Mayor's maid
ELIZABETH JANE	Mayor's daughter
QUASHEBA	Maroon girl plays Queen
CUFFIE	Maroon boy plays Actor Boy Prince
GATHA	Driver's common law wife
	plays Executioner
SLIM	Member of the Jonkunnu band
	plays Jack-in-the Green

Chorus played by members of the cast.

Production History

Maskarade was initially commissioned in 1973 by the Jamaican Information Service for broadcast on television when it was directed by Jim Nelson who subsequently collaborated with the playwright in the expansion of the play which was performed in Cuba in 1979. However this text was re-written for the production directed by Sandra Richards with musical direction by Michael Britt and choreography by Halifu Osumare, at the Nitery, Stanford University Campus in April 1983. In February 1992 it was presented at Northwestern University in the Josephine Louis Theatre directed by Sandra Richards and choreographed by Althea Teamer. In December 1993 it was produced by Talawa Theatre Company at the Cochrane Theatre in London when it was directed by Yvonne Brewster, designed by Ellen Cairns and choreographed by Greta Mendez.

- 'The greatest mind the Caribbean has ever produced'. C.L.R. James on Sylvia Wynter.

- 'A Caribbean intellectual of surpassing originality and brilliance'. David White on Sylvia Wynter, *Small Axe 8* (2000).

- She says: 'Growing up in the then British colony of Jamaica, the anti-colonial uprisings of the mid-to-late 1930s which crossed my childhood were to indelibly mark my life and work. Like *The Hills of Hebron*, the play *Maskarade* was part of the overall creative effort in a now independent British West Indies, to imaginatively create "a new conception of the self"; and thereby, of being human'.

Sylvia Wynter OJ was born in Cuba in 1928. At age two her parents returned to Jamaica where she received her primary and secondary education. In 1946 she was awarded the Jamaica Centenary Scholarship for Girls, which took her to Kings College London to read Modern European Languages.

She was a member of The Boscoe Holder Dance company between 1957-58.

In 1962 the year of Jamaica's Independence her only novel, *The Hills of Hebron* was published.

Her plays include *Maskarade, Under the Sun* (written for the Royal Court Theatre, England), and in 1970 *Rockstone Anancy*, a Jamaican Pantomime.

Among many other publications are a biography of Sir Alexander Bustamante, the first prime minister of independent Jamaica, *Ballad for a Rebellion*, and *We Must Learn to Sit Down Together and Talk About a Little Culture: Reflections on West Indian Writing and Criticism.*

In 1963 Wynter was appointed assistant lecturer in Hispanic literature at the Mona campus of the University of the West Indies. In 1974 she joined the Department of Literature at the University of California San Diego as a visiting professor. She became chairperson of African and Afro-American Studies, and professor of Spanish in the Department of Spanish and Portuguese at Stanford University in 1977-1997, where she is now Professor Emeritus.

Introduction to Maskarade

Sylvia Wynter answers questions put to her
by Yvonne Brewster.

*YB: Your paper 'Jonkunnu in Jamaica: Folklore as Cultural Process'
is a highly regarded academic paper, not a play. How did the
play* Maskarade *come to be written?*

SW: Firstly, it is in no way either an anthropological or an
ethnographic disciplinary paper. It was first written
as an essay for a UNESCO conference on folklore
which explains its non-academic, and instead, politico-
cultural dynamic as a paper... Jim Nelson[1] would have
responded to the paper in the way he did, especially
given the fact that growing up in a then imperial colony
like Jamaica, all things African had been systemically
stigmatized. That is, until the anticolonial movements
initiated the decolonisation of our hitherto British
imperial domesticated consciousnesses. As a theatrical
artist, Nelson would have been attracted to the other
major aspect of what I myself had discovered in writing
the Jonkunnu essay. This is the fact that, as in the English
Morris dancing popular tradition, or indeed, as in the
black American minstrel show, all of which had, like the
African carnival tradition which gave origin to Jonkunnu,
emerged from the immeasurably older, pre-Christian,
pre-monotheistic, pagan religious, earth-centered popular
religions.

As a tradition out of which pagan elements, such as those
still carried over in Catholicism, had come to constitute,
in our modern world, an ecumenically human popular
tradition. One which we find, in contradiction to the
brutal hierarchy of the slave master and the slave, had

---

1   Having read the paper young Jamaican TV director Jim Nelson famously
enthused: 'There is a play in this. Write it for me!' The first production was
a Jamaica Broadcasting Corporation tele-play, which after some directorial
conceptual work by Jim Nelson et al was reproduced as a play for theatre. As
such, it represented Jamaica at the 1979 Carifesta Festival in Cuba.

continued to be syncretized within the terms of what had become in Jamaica, the now matrix African-pagan carnival tradition.

With the result that the popular, farcical doctor plays common to them all had come to syncretically integrate themselves at a popular level, as carried, on the one hand, by the slaves, and on the other, in the case of the English Morris dancing, for example, by the lower bookkeeper overseer classes, who would have been the main carriers of the Anglo-Scottish variant of this tradition. This paradoxically then, as a tradition out of which the now global popular musical culture of the world was to emerge.

YB: *Music plays an essential role in the play. How did you go about deciding on this element?*

SW: This has always seemed to me to be provided by the popular musical tradition, whether in the United States or in Jamaica in its contemporary forms. What Sandra Richards did was use elements from the Jamaican folk tradition as well as from the emergent rap tradition. I would imagine that any version of the play would follow the same formula by incorporating the contemporary popular musical forms.

YB: *The play script of* Maskarade *which appears in this collection is a later edition performed in the USA in 1983. Is there a reason for this choice?*

SW: Originally the Miss Gatha character of the play had been imagined in the same terms as she had originally been in my novel *The Hills of Hebron* (1962). This explains my strong disagreement with Jim Nelson on this single aspect of her being made into the stereotyped figure of the yard woman tradition in the original productions. I felt that this was strongly at variance with the African tradition out of which the Jonkunnu ceremony of the play *Maskarade* had evolved. This especially so with respect to Miss Gatha, whom I had conceived as still embodying the major conception of Mother Earth and of the conception of justice, which is fundamentally different from that of the West's legalistic conception. By the way, the latter itself is a conception of justice that is also completely different from what had been the West's medieval tradition's conception of justice as either that of just or unjust titles, rather than, in our case, completely dependent upon legality and illegality. That is, a conception far more profoundly ethical in its mythological order of things. I must add that most of Nelson's other contributions to the script in the nineteen seventies were in many ways brilliantly innovative.

In the United States, when I was teaching at Stanford University from 1977 onwards, the play was produced by my very dear and talented colleague Sandra Richards, and it was for that production that in 1983 I rewrote the play, envisioning Miss Gatha's later role as the executioner in this alternative, so that it was now wholly my own conception, although the first school edition of the television play, the 1979 edition and my later version are directly correlated.

YB: Maskarade *is regarded as a seminal Jamaican play. It is always in the top three when classical Jamaican plays are discussed. Why do you think it has withstood the test of time and fashion so emphatically?*

SW: Your last question: fundamentally, the play is not mine. It is really my reworking of a millennially extended popular pagan tradition which is universally applicable, and whose formula I have merely copied. So in a sense it doesn't really belong to me; I see myself as merely its transmitter. A major parallel, of course, is the pantomime tradition of both Britain and Jamaica.

ACT ONE

SCENE ONE
ON A HILL ABOVE KINGSTON

SCENE TWO
BRAINSY'S TAILORING SHOP

SCENE THREE
OUTSIDE MAYOR MITCHELL'S HOUSE

SCENE FOUR
ON A HILL ABOVE KINGSTON/BRAINSY'S SHOP

ACT TWO

SCENE ONE
ON A HILL ABOVE KINGSTON/OUTSIDE
MAYOR MITCHELL'S HOUSE

SCENE TWO
ON A HILL ABOVE KINGSTON/DRIVER AND
GATHA'S YARD

SCENE THREE
ON A HILL ABOVE KINGSTON/BRAINSY'S SHOP

SCENE FOUR
BRAINSY'S SHOP/DRIVER AND GATHA'S YARD

ACT THREE

SCENE ONE
ON A HILL ABOVE KINGSTON/
A KINGSTON STREET

Act 1

The orchestra overture ends with Jonkunnu-type drumming, then fades into silence as the curtain rises. The setting is early morning. Backdrop of mountains, tall and shrouded. Lighting to suggest that the mist swirling about the mountains is a continuation in a different modality and in a minor key of the music we have heard. This will be central to the synaesthesia effect i.e. with the senses replicating their effects. The set must catch the opposition of the Blue Mountain, the plains and the sea. The two-level stage serves to mark the difference-interaction of past and present. When the play begins the Jonkunnu Festival (see Appendix) has had to take refuge in the hills; to go underground like the Maroons. This sense of an underground existence needs to be brought out. A rickety sign half-falling, says '17 miles to Kingston'. LOVEY and the BOY wait on the lower level center stage, although the upper level is their turf, so to speak, during the play. They wait expectantly. The BOY listens, hears nothing. Takes up his bamboo flute. Looks up at the mist swirling. Plays a thread of a tune as if in accompaniment. Then he breaks off, alert. His tone is joyful.

BOY: You hear something Mass Lovey?

It's them?

At last?

LOVEY: Only the breeze!

BOY: But…

LOVEY: The breeze play like that
In the bamboo leaves, can sound
Like the walk a man walk.

BOY: *(Impatient.)* But why they take so long?
I tired to wait, man! Cho!

LOVEY: It's a long way to have to come.
All the way up from the sea
Up past Half-Way Tree, then turn

Up past Papine.

BOY: It's a long way!

LOVEY: And on top of that they have
   To sneak like a thief,
   Hush drum, quiet dance
   Still fife, out torch
   So that the law don't hear!
   So that the law don't see!
   They have to run like a stream
   That run under the ground, till
   She find the sea and splash
   Out into the sun.

BOY: Ever since that time?

   To dub, chants.

LOVEY: Ever since that time.
   Ever since Jonkunnu maskarade ban by law.
   In Kingston town
   They have to come all that way
   To dance Jonkunnu!

BOY: Up past Parade, up past cross-roads
   Up past Half-Way Tree
   Turn up past Papine?

LOVEY: All that way till
   They turn up the hills
   Till they break free!

BOY: It's still a long time to wait!

LOVEY: We can use the time to practice.
   Get the fife.

BOY: I will never learn it,
   My tongue always tie up.

LOVEY: You will learn.
   After you practice over and over,

Till your face, your eye,

Your finger and your feet

Have their own mind, keep their own time.

Till your tongue leap light and spin and gleam

In the silence of the sea!

Then you'll be a master of mime,

A teller of tales and a spinner of dreams.

BOY: Like you, Mass Lovey?

LOVEY: Like me, you ready?

BOY: From the beginning again?

LOVEY: From the beginning!

The BOY plays a fanfare on the fife. The orchestra repeats. As he narrates, a new dubbing theme, different from LOVEY's, accompanies. LOVEY's dub and the BOY's dub will counterpoint.

BOY: Come one, come all

Come high, come low,

Come and see our ballad show!

Come close, sit down.

Listen while I relate

A terrible place of love and hate

That took place in Kingston Town

In the year of our Lord

Eighteen Hundred and Forty-One.

LOVEY's dub begins.

LOVEY: Then as now,

I was a teller of tales

Gathering pennies,

Selling dreams.

BOY: Lovey the Great

Spinner of dreams

Master of mime

Teller of tales

On a Kingston street.

LOVEY: I was eye witness
> To the spectacle.

> *The tempo on the fife quickens. The BOY mimes the action.*

> Blow for Blow,
> Lead for Lead,
> Blood for Blood
> Actor Boy King
> And Actor Boy Prince
> Stone cold dead on a Kingston street.
> After that, riot! Soldier! Gun!
> I remember well, how I remember well.
> That Christmas Jonkunnu Maskarade,
> The people, the tale,
> And the part we all played.

> *He interrupts himself, as though overhearing someone in the audience whispering.*

> Now some people might think, say
> That the tale I going to tell
> Just a nice little piece of 'ethnic' business!
> So let me warn you from the beginning
> I'm no folklore Uncle Remus
> With a fake lore masquerade
> For some of you to come and get
> Your doctorate on!

BOY: Not a damn!
> The tale we going to tell
> Trace its pedigree
> Way back from when

LOVEY: The first line trace
> On the first rock face.

BOY: The first tool make!

LOVEY: The first mask dance
> The first drum beat.

BOY: Long before Sumer
Egypt or Crete
Long before Babylon
Genesis or Greece!

LOVEY: Long before then!
With the first tale
That man tell of himself!

BOY: And it's our task now
To carry on

LOVEY: That first invent
That man invent.

BOY: Himself! Herself! Ourself!

LOVEY: So that the separate flesh
Could feel as one
Could live as one
Could share as one.

BOY: Once nature stop.

LOVEY: And history begin!

Change of dub tone: Brisk, matter-of-fact.

BOY: So now that we get
That straight
Listen while we set the stage
For our terrible tale
Of Love and Hate!

Shift to storytelling beat. LOVEY will tell his story in the style of a calypsonian, i.e. driving, rhythmic, fast-paced. His dub becomes the parallel of a calypso or reggae beat. The stage jumps with rhythmic excitement with the rhythm as dominant as the words.

LOVEY: It was a cold December month
December, 1841, the wind
Cut through the Kingston streets
Like knife on ice.

Mayor Hector Mitchell
Wake up on the wrong side of his bed,
So his temper wasn't nice!

BOY: Nice! How Mayor temper
Could nice, when
His business near bankrupt,
His sourface wife,
Cripple in bed upstairs.
His daughter downstairs
Like wild bird in cage?

LOVEY: So he warn us strong
That morning of eighteen
Forty-one when he wake up on
The wrong side of his bed!
He warn us well!

The Mayor's dub takes over here as the BOY mimes the Mayor's part and the CHORUS responds as the Crowd.

BOY: I am a tough tough Mayor
Of world wide renown
I don't fool around
You know me well!

CHORUS: Yes, Mayor Mitchell sir!
We know you well!

BOY: I am out to show this town, once and for all!
I am the Order, I am the Law!
I am out to show this town
What I say, go!

CHORUS: Show it sir! Show it!

BOY: I want you ignorant idlers of Kingston
To understand one fact!
Too many Jonkunnu band
Every Christmas Festival
Making scandal in Kingston

Catching fight, this band with that one!
Busting head, bleeding blood
Making noise in decent people head!
Stop it! Or feel my iron hand!
You hear me! You understand?

CHORUS: *(Sings.)* Mayor, we hear you, we hear you well!
We must behave weself, we hear you well!
You out fe war, edo edo, you out fe war.
Behave weself, or Jonkunnu dead!

As they sing, the BOY changes his persona as Mayor, changing props, etc. back to his apprentice role. As the song ends he comes forward. The BOY's dub now.

BOY: It was into this situation
That Actor-Boy Number One
Enter the equation
Set the whole story into motion!

Fanfare.

I give you Ladies
I give you Gentlemen
Actor Boy Number One!
Driver by Name
Driver by occupation!

DRIVER, elegant in Coachman's outfit enters to fanfare – strikes pose downstage.

LOVEY: Now Driver was a Kingston man,
A scuffler if ever there was one!
He drive a carriage for Mayor Mitchell
As his regular employment.
But come every Christmas
He put out a maskarade band,
Scuffle a little extra money.
Driver's Jonkunnu band is the best band in Kingston.

BOY: No band could beat that band!

LOVEY: Now Driver organize
  The Band all right
  But his friend Brainsy
  Dance Pitchie Patchie fool in Jonkunnu
  And is the brains behind the band!

BRAINSY enters, in a tumbling somersault, dressed in Tailor's outfit. Strikes pose, doing business, etc. with cloth draped on Tailor's dummy.

LOVEY: Brainsy plan the costume.
  Cut them out, sew them
  With the help of a Deaf-Mute
  His apprentice who dance, and prance
  Houseboat in Jonkunnu!

DEAF-MUTE, dressed as a Tailor's apprentice, enters with great leaps and twirls, than sits on stool, also engaged in business, etc. in Tailor's shop.

LOVEY: Oh that was a band that Jonkunnu band!
  Never any band to beat that one!
  With Actor Boy King
  Actor Boy Prince.

The BOY mimes the characters of the folk play.

LOVEY: And the fight that they fight
  For the thone, for the Queen
  For the Kingdom!
  How they could dance and mime!
  How they could fight
  And die
  And rise to fight again!
  How they could spin a tale!
  Like a rainbow stain
  Shimmering on a Kingston street
  After rain.

Shift of music/mood. Brisk, everyday day.

BOY: So when you see a date in your history book
  1841, Mayor Mitchell abolish Jonkunnu
  Ban it from Kingston and its environs
  Take note there's something personal behind it.
  For is man make history,
  And is Driver cause it!

LOVEY: *(To a fast-paced rhythm: dub.)*
  For that year
  Trouble take Driver
  In his old age!
  From the time his eye
  Fall on a pretty maid
  Down at Parade!
  One turn she turn her eye up
  One turn she turn them down!
  From that time on
  Love strike like earthquake!
  Driver drive on
  But from that time on
  He lost his heart
  And he lost his way!

  DRIVER moves out of his pose but stands bemused.

BOY: Love strike Driver dead,
  Love strike for true!
  Love turn Driver from super-fly
  Into fool!

  Lights off BOY and LOVEY, up on Tailor's shop. DRIVER goes to mirror, turns viewing himself. A chant of CHORUS offstage could be used while the scene is being shifted.

CHORUS: Strike him love
  Let him know that life
  Is not no puppet show
  No moonshine doll
  You play joke with

You take step with
You do as you have the mind with!
Let him know that life
Have another face that hide
Behind the harsh
White light of noon
Let him see that other side, love
Let him see it – soon!

SCENE 2

Lights fully up on BRAINSY's tailoring shop, cluttered with bits of costume for the coming masquerade. DEAF-MUTE works diligently at decorating the Queen's Throne. BRAINSY sits sewing. DRIVER tries on the Horsehead costume and examines himself in the mirror. Shakes his head. Snatches off the Horsehead.

DRIVER: *(Explosive.)* You know something, Brainsy?
   I tired of playing horsehead year in, year out,
   Making an ass of myself,
   I born for better part than that, man.
   Something that express the real me.
   Something with power, authority, weight
   I going back to play Actor Boy King.

   BRAINSY laughs quietly without looking up.

DRIVER: So what so funny?

BRAINSY: You look at yourself in the glass?

DRIVER: *(Looking.)* Well I'm a little fat here and there
   Put on a little weight these few years.
   So what? King can't fat?

BRAINSY: *(Holding up small King's costume.)* King can fat,
   But not King costume!
   What you want me do with this?
   Let out a few yard here and there?

DRIVER: So what,
   You can't cut new costume?

You can't sew new cloth?

BRAINSY: Cut new costume! Sew new cloth!

Driver don't make me vex

Don't draw my tongue!

Don't year after year I keep telling you?

Year after year till I tired

I tell you we need

To invest in new costume

If we not to

Keep on falling year after year

Behind the other band!

If we to keep on coaxing

Money out of people hand!

Over and over I tell you

If we want to make money

We have to spend money!

DRIVER: But that's what…

BRAINSY: *(Not listening. Angrily, sweeps the costumes to the floor.)*
Call this costume? This is old cloth!

Not even dead man would see himself

Dead in this one!

You don't see, Driver man?

We need more glitter, we need more spangle

We need new bead, we need new bangle

We need more pomp, or we might as well done with the band.

DRIVER puts his hand over BRAINSY's mouth and forcibly sits him down.

DRIVER: Cover your mouth, open

Your ears. Listen, I Driver

I – Man take a decision!

I going to invest! At last! In new costume!

…Look!

He takes out a cloth bag, pours coins on table. BRAINSY takes one up reverently, rings it against another then tests it with his teeth.

BRAINSY: Money! New Costume!

Now Lettest Thou Thy

Servant depart in peace!

My eyes have seen the glory

Of Driver's hand, letting go money!

DRIVER: Don't play joke, man!

Now look – *(He separates some of the coins.)*

This is for my costume as

Actor Boy, the King.

I want it extra special,

First class, to express that real man

That people never see when

They first look at me!

And let go your hand, spend

Money the way you want to all these years!

Let go your hand!

BRAINSY beckons to DEAF-MUTE who brings him his sketching pad.

BRAINSY: You know something Driver?

If you really serious

I have a new way to make your King's costume.

I see some new satin cloth at Feurtado,

A rich, rich purple

I would make the breeches like this

…and like this

…and like this.

The jacket like this

Long lines to slim you down

The sleeves to lend you authority

Like this… *(He sketches.)*

DRIVER: *(Putting out more money.)* Now this is a costume for Quasheba.

Twice for her costume what I give you for mine.

I want a costume for Quasheba

That will sweep her off her feet.

Money no object.

BRAINSY: *(Still sketching.)* Costume for Quash what, Quash-who?

Change of lighting. DRIVER changes mood. Reggae music under.

DRIVER: Quasheba!

My Queen of Sheba.

BRAINSY: *(Puzzled, all attention now.)* Your… What?

DRIVER: *(Serious.)* She is the last knock

I knock on the door, Brainsy!

The last ask, I ask from life

The first see I see her

Lightning strike!

Lights upon BRAINSY as he signals to DEAF-MUTE to bring a bottle of rum and glasses: DEAF-MUTE pours, BRAINSY gives to DRIVER.

BRAINSY: Cool it Driver. Pour

Some white rum down.

Cool down the fever.

Then tell me what the hell

You killing yourself up for

Over this Quash-who

Quash-what!

DRIVER: *(Drinks.)* When you see her

You will understand

Brainsy, man.

When you see how her

Breast point like Blue Mountain

Her face like Poinciana flower

Her laugh like Yallah's River

Her waist like bamboo stem!

You will see

When I bring her

For you to take measurement
For her new costume.

BRAINSY stops cutting. Seats himself. Takes up his own drink. He will sit still as DRIVER acts out his narration, with DEAF-MUTE playing the part of QUASHEBA. The narration will be done in ballad style and must be fast-paced. The orchestra will intervene from time to time to provide sounds like the carriage horses, raucous satirical sounds accompanying BRAINSY's comments. The orchestra keeps a reggae beat under the scene, pacing it.

BRAINSY: Alright Driver, explain yourself
Tell me what new scheme
You scheming now, and how
The same scheme this time
Different from all other time?

DRIVER: Yesterday I drop off Mayor Mitchell
At his counting house.
And as I turn the carriage
Around the corner of Parade
My eye light on this maid!
And I tell you something!
Lightning strike me!

BRAINSY: Like all the other time!

DRIVER: This time special!
I sense that this time
I have to take care.
So I take time to ease the carriage
Clip clop clip clop after her.
By the time I reach West Parade
She realize it's she I following.
She turn around, turn her eye up
Then give a little come-on smile.
But by the time I whoa the horse
Jump down to talk to her
She turn into a lane

Then into a yard and gone!

BRAINSY: The peadove fly away?

DRIVER: Fly away but after that smile
    I know to myself
    She mean me to wait.
    So I wait.

BRAINSY: And what happen?

DRIVER: I wait…

BRAINSY: So you wait? Then what?

DRIVER: Little time after, you should
    See her Brainsy, tiptoe back
    Come stand just inside the gate
    Pretending is not me
    She looking at…
    She come right back, just as
    I expect, perch there like peadove
    Waiting for hunter gun
    To take aim!

BRAINSY: And you take aim
    And say to yourself
    Mark!
    And you fire? Pam!
    Peadove flutter down
    Into your hand!

DRIVER: Not so easy as that
    This story like all story
    Have a little complication.

Lights down on DRIVER and BRAINSY as CHORUS sings, and one of the masquerade group dressed as a Bird is hunted by DEAF-MUTE in mime and dance.

CHORUS: *(Sings.)* Mister Driver go fe hunt peadove wallo,
    wallo, wallo, wallo
    He meet up with another hunter on the way

Wallo, wallo, wallo

Mr Driver come here the other day

Fe go hunt peadove edoh

Mister Driver come here the other day

But the peadove fly away.

Repeat. Male/female dance duet re. hunter and peadove.

SCENE 3

Outside Mayor Mitchell's house. By the front door, MAUD, the Servant, is a woman of about thirty with a cap and apron and is dusting the gilded frame of a large portrait of Mayor Mitchell in his Mayor's gown. Later she will kneel and clean and shine the floor with a coconut brush. She will work steadily, groaning to herself, through the scene. Mayor Mitchell's daughter ELIZABETH JANE is seated on a stone bench by the front door. She is about 16. Fair-haired. Pretty. Dressed in fashion of the time. With much care. She holds an embroidery frame and is embroidering a pillow case for her hope chest. The hope chest, a large mahogany one, stands under Mayor Mitchell's portrait. When MAUD dusts the portrait, she stands on it. Then kneels to polish it. QUASHEBA, about the same age, slender, tall, grave, beautiful, wearing the old-fashioned dress of a rural peasant, enters. She stands awkwardly.

QUASHEBA: Good morning please, ma'am. *(To MAUD.)* Good
    morning.

MAUD: What you want?

QUASHEBA: I came to see Mister Driver ma'am.

MAUD: Driver don't live here

    Driver only work here.

    What you come to see him for?

QUASHEBA: He tell me to meet him here ma'am,

    Today, to make arrangements

    About the Jonkunnu play.

MAUD: Well, this is Mayor Mitchell's house

    And Mayor Mitchell front door

If you want to see Driver
Go to the back gate and wait there.

QUASHEBA: Thank you, ma'am. *(She makes to go off.)*
You could do me a favour, ma'am?

MAUD: What?

QUASHEBA: Cuffie, ma'am, my friend
You could tell him when he come
That I am waiting at the back.

MAUD: Why should I do that?
I am Mayor Mitchell's servant
I not here to pass on message
To any stranger.
This is private people place
Not a railway station...

ELIZABETH JANE: What's your name?

QUASHEBA: I name Quasheba ma'am.

ELIZABETH JANE: What kind of a name is that?

MAUD: Quashie, you mean?

QUASHEBA: No ma'am. Quasheba.
Cuffie say that long ago
In Africa before our old time people
Come across the salt water
Akwasiba was the name for a girl born on Sunday
And up in Portland where Cuffie and my
Grandmother come from
They still use that name!
She did name Quasheba
And she pass her name on to me
She was a Maroon
Like Cuffie.

MRS MITCHELL's voice is heard offstage. She bangs her walking stick on the floor throughout this scene.

MRS MITCHELL: Elizabeth Jane?

ELIZABETH JANE: Who is Cuffie?

QUASHEBA: My boyfriend, ma'am.
> But he is a Maroon too
> And he say the Maroons
> Call him the African way.
> They call him Kofi and…

MRS MITCHELL: Elizabeth Jane?

MAUD shoos ELIZABETH JANE offstage.

MAUD: What you a come with
> 'Bout your Akwasiba and Kofi?
> You name Quashie and Cuffie
> Like every other stupid country bumpkin!
> 'Bout your Maroon grandmother
> And your Maroon boyfriend
> As if Maroon is anything special
> As if Maroon not maugre dog just like
> Every other black people them.

MRS MITCHELL: Maud? Maud?

MAUD: Coming this minute, Mrs Mitchell, ma'am. Coming this minute.
> And get your dirty self
> Out of decent white people yard!

MRS MITCHELL: Maud!!

ELIZABETH JANE re-enters in time to hear last remark.

ELIZABETH JANE: My mother want you upstairs this minute!

MRS MITCHELL: Maud!

ELIZABETH JANE: Quasheba! Don't pay her no mind
> You can come back.
> Her bark worse than her bite.

The song of 'Jane and Louise' begins on the fife. Total change of mood, as if a cloud has gone from the scene. The two young girls about the same age play a scene as if they were still children, before race and class differences had separated them.

ELIZABETH JANE: My name is Elizabeth Jane

My grandmother named me after her too.

But you can call me Miss Elizabeth like everybody else.

You have a middle name?

QUASHEBA: Louisa, ma'am.

That name after my other grandmother

That one is not a Maroon.

ELIZABETH JANE: Jane and Louisa!

You know the song

You know the game?

QUASHEBA: Yes, ma'am.

ELIZABETH JANE: Come, let's play it.

Let us pretend

It still is now

The way it was then…

ELIZABETH JANE gets up, puts down her sewing. They face each other, hands on hips. They sway to the waltz tune, singing and playing the game. Drum and fife accompaniment.

QUASHEBA and ELIZABETH JANE: *(Sing.)* Jane and Louisa

Will soon come home

Oh will soon come home

Oh will soon come home

Into this beautiful garden…

They mime the actions of the song.

My love will you allow me

To pick a rose

Oh to pick a rose

Into this beautiful garden.

They change the rhythm to a brisk one and clap and chant.

Jane and Louisa born on a Sunday

Whom will they marry?
Try and tell me!

QUASHEBA and ELIZABETH JANE: Jane and Louisa will soon
come home
Will soon come home
Will soon come home
Jane and Louisa will soon come home
Into this beautiful garden.

My love will you allow me to pick a rose
To pick a rose
To pick a rose
My love will you allow me to pick a rose
Into this beautiful garden?

Jane and Louisa born on a Sunday
Born on Sunday
Born on Sunday
Who, oh who will they marry?

QUASHEBA: Will he be rich?

ELIZABETH JANE: Will he be poor?

QUASHEBA: Will he be young?

ELIZABETH JANE: Will he be old?

BOTH: You turn to the left
You turn to the right
You wheel and turn
And shut your eyes tight
You open your eyes and that will be.
The very very one that he will be.

They wheel, wheel, open their eyes. See no one, and laugh.

ELIZABETH JANE: You see anyone, Quasheba?

QUASHEBA: Only a Johncrow! You see anyone, ma'am?

ELIZABETH JANE: Only a pitcheri!

ELIZABETH JANE seats herself on the bench. QUASHEBA seats herself on a small stool. ELIZABETH JANE fans herself with the embroidery – still laughing.

It's really a Johncrow I see

You know Quasheba…

(Whispers.) It's really a Johncrow

I going to marry?

QUASHEBA: You going to married, ma'am?

ELIZABETH JANE: *(Puts her fingers to her lips, glances at the upstairs window.)*

Sh…h. My mother not supposed to know.

My father arrange it.

QUASHEBA: But how come your mother don't know, ma'am?

ELIZABETH JANE: She is a cripple and can't come downstairs

So she don't know half of what going on…

QUASHEBA: But you don't tell your mother, ma'am?

That you going to married?

ELIZABETH JANE: You tell your mother 'bout your boyfriend Cuffie?

QUASHEBA: My mother dead and buried just after I born, ma'am

And my grandmother raise me

But Cuffie did ask her for me

Before she dead, and she said yes…

ELIZABETH JANE: Your story different from mine.

My mother wouldn't say yes

If they crucify her

Yes, to the half-black man my father

Want me married to.

She beckons her to come and sit beside her. QHASHEBA does so.

ELIZABETH JANE: *(Whispering.)* The whole of Kingston know about it, but my

Father want to keep it secret from my mother

Until after the wedding over and done with.
You see, the man is going to put money in my
Father's business so it can save.
His wife died last year
And she didn't give him any children
So he want to marry me
To try one more time.
(She laughs.) But he so old you see Quasheba!

QUASHEBA laughs.

QUASHEBA: Then why you want to married to him. To take
him make joke?

ELIZABETH JANE: My father want it!
Not me.

QUASHEBA: But how <u>you</u> feel 'bout it Miss Elizabeth?

ELIZABETH JANE: Cho! I just glad to get
Away from this house
And from my mother
She is a miserable old bitch!
An old higue!

QUASHEBA: *(Shocked.)* Don't talk like that about
Your mother ma'am
God will curse you!

ELIZABETH JANE: You don't know my mother, Quasheba.
That's why I going to marry
Old Moses Campbell.
To get away from her!
And to see her face
When she hear about the wedding!
And that my husband
Is a half-black man!

QUASHEBA: You like him, ma'am?
Even a little bit?

ELIZABETH JANE: Not even a little bit.

But he spend his money like water on me!

He open an account at all the Kingston stores

And I buy everything my eye light on!

Indian silk at Nathan's and ruby earrings and silk shawls at Fuertado...

And look, look at the ring.

She takes a shawl, the earrings and a ring from a bag, drapes the shawl about her shoulders, then begins to put them on.

QUASHEBA: The ring pretty for true!

And the earrings and the shawl

I like the feel of the silk.

She feels the shawl.

ELIZABETH JANE: I have to hide everything downstairs

So my mother won't see.

What Cuffie give you?

QUASHEBA: *(Slowly, as if realizing it for the first time.)* Cuffie don't have anything to give...

ELIZABETH JANE: Then what you marrying him for then?

QUASHEBA: *(Slowly.)* Well...my grandmother did say yes when he did ask her for me and...

Well...

ELIZABETH JANE: Well, what?

QUASHEBA: Well, it just like all of a sudden,

I blaze up ma'am, like dry leaf fire

In August sun.

ELIZABETH JANE: I did feel like that once.

Just like that. Like I was just blazing

And blazing and I wanted to stop

And I couldn't stop...

Pause.

My mother make us stop. *(Pause. Fife begins.)*

He come up into my room

47

Like I tell him to, late at night.
Maud hear us, wake my mother
My mother come in and catch us.

QUASHEBA: She catch you?

ELIZABETH JANE: He was the gardener man son
And they make the gardener man
Beat him half to death. *(Pause.)*
They send him away to the country
Where the gardener man come from. *(Pause.)*
I never feel like that again
Since they lost him away
In Portland mountain!

Pause. Fife continues 'Jane and Louisa' theme.

QUASHEBA: *(Seeking for something to say to dispel the mood.)*
That's where Cuffie come from ma'am,
Portland mountain.
And I come from the sea
Near Port Antonio.

ELIZABETH JANE: I know Port Antonio.
We drive through there
When I used to go and spend
Holidays on my grandmother's
Property in the country.
I use to love it there you see.
Up here in town
My mother corset me.
But in the country I live free.
In the country at Christmas
I even jump Jonkunnu.

QUASHEBA: Jonkunnu, ma'am!

ELIZABETH JANE: The children of the people
Who work on my grandmother's land
And me at Christmas, we get up

A Jonkunnu band
And I dance the Queen...see.

Jonkunnu music. ELIZABETH JANE dances as Queen. MAUD returns. She stands with her broom, watching.

QUASHEBA: I going to play Queen, too, ma'am.

This Christmas I going
To play Queen in Mr Driver
Jonkunnu band...see.

She joins ELIZABETH JANE. They dance.

A VOICE OFF: *(Stern.)* Elizabeth Jane.

ELIZABETH JANE stops at once. So does QUASHEBA.

VOICE: Elizabeth Jane, don't you hear me calling you?

ELIZABETH JANE: Yes, Mama.

ELIZABETH JANE slowly takes up her embroidery, and begins to hum 'Jane and Louisa' mutinously.

VOICE: How many times must I tell you
Not to wrap up with these
No good worthless black people?

ELIZABETH JANE stops her ears and keeps humming softly. She signals to QUASHEBA to do the same.

And out there burning up
Your white skin in the sun!
You want to lose your chance
To marry off to an English gentleman
With future, money, prospects
Make your home in England
And leave this black people land
Come inside I tell you!
Come inside from the sun!

ELIZABETH JANE with her hands over her ears, her embroidery on her head, and still humming goes inside.

QUASHEBA: *(Singing softly to herself.)* My love will you allow
me

To pick a rose

Oh to pick a rose

Into this beautiful garden!

*CUFFIE has entered behind her. He comes up and puts his hand
over her eyes.*

QUASHEBA: Cuffie?

CUFFIE: *(Taking his hands away.)* Who else?

*They take hands and waltz as if still in the children's game.
QUASHEBA sings softly as they sway, holding hands. He looks at
her, not singing, but entering her mood. The fife picks up the tune,
and the CHORUS sings.*

CHORUS and QUASHEBA: My love will you allow me

To waltz with you

Oh to waltz with you

My love will you allow me to waltz with you

Into this beautiful garden.

*CUFFIE and QUASHEBA walk off, swinging hands, in time to
the song.*

CHORUS and QUASHEBA: My love will you allow me to pick
a rose

To pick a rose, to pick a rose

My love will you allow me to pick a rose

Into this beautiful garden.

My love will you allow me to waltz with you

To waltz with you, to waltz with you

My love will you allow me to waltz with you

Into this beautiful garden.

SCENE 4

LOVEY: *(To audience and CHORUS. Dub.)*

What Driver don't know

With all his plot and plan

Is that Cuffie enter
Quasheba garden already!
Cuffie pick Quasheba rose
Already and
Like a bee that sip
Honey and drunk on it
Cuffie tie to Quasheba
Like drunk man
Tie to rum bottle!

BOY: Cuffie enter Quasheba garden
Cuffie pick Quasheba rose! First!

LOVEY: Driver blind his eye
Don't want to know
That is how the story go!

BOY: Driver see the peadove
He cry mark. He aim!
He fire! Pam!

LOVEY: But he keep his back turn.
And don't see
The other hunter
That did mark the dove
That did aim first!
And fire! Pam!

BOY: The other hunter
That did stake his claim!
Before the Driver even mark the dove!

The lights go up on BRAINSY's shop. The latter is measuring DRIVER. DRIVER is holding in his waist, with great effort.

BRAINSY: If you don't let out your breath
And I make the tunic too tight
One slash you slash the stick, the tunic rip!

DRIVER hastily lets out his breath.

BRAINSY: *(As he measures.)* You can go on with your story now.
What this complication 'bout?

Drums and dub under the narration that DRIVER gives, so that it's like a production number rather than strictly a mere 'realistic' scene, with DRIVER talking and miming to the rhythmic beat.

DRIVER: Let me tell you first
How we start out the negotiation
Before we stumble on the complication.
Now, Deaf-Mute, you are Quasheba.

He puts a shawl around DEAF-MUTE.

And I am Mr Driver, deck out
In all the splendour
Of Mayor Mitchell's driver!
Seated high up in the carriage.

He puts on his tail coat, his top hat, his boots, takes his gloves, his whip. He and DEAF-MUTE mime the scene.

DRIVER: She stand there inside the gate
Seeing every move I make. So I start the act!
First, I take off my gloves, then
I put one back on, the right hand one.
Then I take that hand and lift my hat
And catch her eye. I look straight at her:
I don't blink.
<u>Later</u>, I say to her. Not one word else.
Then I drive off.

BRAINSY: But if you drive off
That negotiation
Seem like if it is conclusion?

DRIVER: Hold your horse. Not so fast.
That was only scene one.
I wait that night until moonlight
Paper everything in silver
For scene two to take place.

I drive slow – clip clop
Clip clop past her gate –
And I clip the clop so she could hear
Then I turn back and find her
Waiting there as I know
She would wait…

BRAINSY: How you know she would
Come out?

DRIVER: Other people study for doctor
You study for tailor
I study for woman hunter.

BRAINSY: So what happen after that?

DRIVER: I just bend my little finger
And she come up in the carriage
And we drive clip clip clop
Way out of the dirty lane
Right along Palisadoes
Right along the sea.

BRAINSY: And the sea-breeze and the moonlight
And the clip clop, and the luxury of the carriage
Work the trick!
Tricknology! You have
Your doctorate in it.

DRIVER: When I tell you her eye light up!
She nestle into the seat and stroke
The velvet curtain with her fingers
And when I make the horse gallop
She hold onto me tight tight
And laugh with delight
And wrinkle her face like kitten
And I feel her body, tight
Next to me.
And I know this was it!

BRAINSY: *(Breaks rhythm)* Like all the other it?

DRIVER: This is a different it
　　　From all the other ones
　　　But how you to know?
　　　You never love yet.

BRAINSY: *(Dryly)* No.

DRIVER: Don't let it get you down
　　　Brainsy, is nothing to do with you.
　　　The way I look at it God make people as if
　　　He cast them for a role
　　　In Jonkunnu maskarade.
　　　Give every one part to play
　　　That suit them!
　　　Now look at you!
　　　Is plain God cast you
　　　To play the fool, and everybody
　　　Agree, Brainsy the tailor
　　　Is the best Pitchie Patchie
　　　Of any Jonkunnu band in Kingston.

DEAF-MUTE who has been reading DRIVER's lips, nods enthusiastically, Jonkunnu music under as he dances and mimes like Pitchie Patchie, using the latter's whip.

DRIVER: You see! Even Deaf-Mute says yes.
　　　Pitchie Patchie suit you down to the ground
　　　And you play the part well.
　　　But the problem is this.
　　　How you expect any woman
　　　To fall in love with a fool?

BRAINSY: Then how they fall in love with you?
　　　What role God cast you for?

DRIVER: A king, Brainsy.
　　　The kind of king who don't win
　　　War with gun, but win it

At the negotiations
After the war come.

BRAINSY: That's what you catch the women
With then? Your negotiations?

DRIVER: Go to the head of the class!
In my own way, I am an artist.
The same science
You put into sewing,
Is the same science I put into
Hunting woman.
And, Brainsy, let Dr Driver
Give you lesson number one
When you go to hunt a peadove
To get her out the bush
Into your hand, you have to
Know how to play her
The way a master-drummer
Play a Jonkunnu drum!

Jonkunnu drums. Fast rhythm. DEAF-MUTE mimes QUASHEBA
as DRIVER illustrates.

DRIVER: You have to know just how to beat
The rhythm, soft, tough
Slow quick, slow rough, quick, quick, quick…

BRAINSY: Alright! So you catch another one
You prove you are a hell of a man!
So what?
You catch her, have her, tired of her
Then dash her 'way like banana skin.
It's time you start to act your age!
Every time bucket go to well
One day, one of them young gal
Going to pull you so deep you drown!

DRIVER: This not any young gal

       This time special!

       She make me feel that

       At last everything add up.

BRAINSY: How you make her feel?

       A young girl like that?

       What you have to offer

       To blind her eye with?

DRIVER: *(He seats himself on the throne.)* I have a throne, Brainsy.

       A Jonkunnu kingdom and

       Crown of gold. And she want one thing more

       Than anything else in the world.

       She want to be Jonkunnu

       Queen!

       That's the offer

       I have to give.

BRAINSY: What the hell you mean

       Have?

DRIVER: *(Interrupting.)* I going to dress her in the finest Queen outfit

       You ever make!... People going to swoon

       When they see it.

BRAINSY: But...?

DRIVER: You can open your hand and spend

       Like water. Money no object.

       Velvet, satin, silver star

       Sprinkle all over her frock

       Gold earrings for her ears

       Silk shoes and gloves to match!

       Show what you can do!

       Show the world what you make of... *(Pause.)*

       What happen? You can't make frock

       Like that? *(Pause.)* Chance like this

       Don't drop in your lap everyday...

BRAINSY: *(Torn.)* That's not it Driver!
>And you know it.
>If you make this young girl Queen
>What about Miss Gatha?

DRIVER: What 'bout her?

BRAINSY: Good God, Driver! How can you ask me that?
>Who in this damn town
>Don't know Agatha Franklin
>Ten years now the best Queen in any
>Jonkunnu band in Kingston!
>People still call her name
>When they talk 'bout Jonkunnu…

DRIVER: That was a few years back.
>You shut up here in your shop
>Don't hear the word going round!
>Queen not what Queen was
>People say!
>Agatha Franklin did pretty once
>But she over the hill now!

BRAINSY: Then what, you just going to
>Turn her out to pasture?
>Like that?
>Ten years add up to something.

DRIVER: Ten years add up in another way!
>*(Pause.)* To tell you the truth
>I still don't understand what happen
>Nor how it turn out so!
>But you see her for yourself.
>Gatha turn sour! *(Pause.)*
>Like life disappoint her
>So she take it out on me.
>Some time we don't exchange
>Two word for the day.

BRAINSY: Perhaps if you did have children…?

DRIVER: Like she didn't really want any!
　　I never see woman like that!
　　Just wrap herself 'bout me
　　Expect me to do the same…
　　(Pause.) After the first time I carry
　　On with a little girl, and I see
　　She take it hard, I tell her honest:
　　Gatha don't invest yourself in me!
　　Connect up yourself
　　With other people!
　　Take one of your friend Maud's children.
　　Go to church, become church sister,
　　Fall in love with the parson
　　Like other women… *(Pause.)*
　　But it was no use… *(Pause.)* Like I talk to a wall.
　　(Pause.) So what she expect me to do?
　　I can't change for her. *(Pause.)*
　　So when it happen about three more time
　　Like she just change overnight!
　　Day in, day out she
　　Just sit in the chair and rock
　　And wait for me to come back
　　Fix me with her eyes like stone. *(Pause.)*
　　As if the whole thing is my fault!
　　That life didn't turn out
　　The way <u>she</u> want!

BRAINSY: If you take away her chance
　　To play Queen it will be worse!

DRIVER: It can't be worse than it is now!
　　A man would have to be made out of sugar
　　To stand up to her bile!
　　She get old and second hand
　　And she know it! The crowd know it too!

That's why we not drawing crowd with
Our Jonkunnu the way we used to!
You just wait and see what a difference
It will make if we get
A new Queen!
If Quasheba say yes
To the proposition I put to her
Last night.

BRAINSY: If she have to sleep
On the great woman-hunter
Proposition, like you having difficulty?

DRIVER: No difficulty, man! Not me!
Just a little stumbling block
A little complication
With the boyfriend that
Trying to make out with her already.

BRAINSY: Wallo. Another hunter call out <u>Mark</u>:
Take aim. Stake his claim!

DRIVER: My plan is to circumvent
That problem
Spoil his aim and steal his claim.
He had a Jonkunnu Band and
They come from Portland
To seek fame and fortune
So I tell her to offer him
To join his Jonkunnu band
With the best Jonkunnu band
In Kingston.

BRAINSY: *(Angry.)* But how you could do
A thing like that
Without consulting me? What the rass
You think it is at all?
The Jonkunnu band
Don't belong to you

For you to do as you please with?
How come we know if
This country bumpkin band
Can jump Jonkunnu?

DRIVER: We not going give most of them
Any big part, man.
They just fill out the scene
Help out the numbers.

BRAINSY: And the boyfriend going
Content with that?

DRIVER: I have a cure for that sore too.
I tell her to offer him,
What no sane man
Can refuse. Tell him
I tell her, that he
Can play Actor-Boy
Number Two.

BRAINSY: The Prince?
Then what the hell part
Slim going to play?
Like you give way
The whole maskarade
And don't ask me a word 'bout it?

DRIVER: Cool it, Brainsy.
Think what's in it for you.
As for Slim as long
As he gets the same pay
It won't matter to him
What part he play!
And the same with
Ratsy!

BRAINSY: So you have it
All cut and dry?

DRIVER: Cut and dry, seal and sign,
>   All ready to deliver!
>   Jonas gone to country
>   And fall sick
>   Slim can play his part
>   As Executioner. As for Ratsy
>   He always wanted to
>   Play Horsehead and
>   Take over from me.
>   And since Marcus joining Church
>   And turn his back on Jonkunnu,
>   Gatha can play Jack-of-the-Green
>   And help you collect
>   The money.

BRAINSY gets up, disturbed.

BRAINSY: I don't like it, Driver!
>   Miss Gatha…going to raise
>   Worse than hell!

DEAF-MUTE nods dolefully.

DRIVER: She can raise all the hell she want!
>   See if I care! I only have one worry
>   And that is how to work it out
>   So that before the make-believe over
>   And Quasheba eye open,
>   I can hit the mark!
>   That's where your part come in…

BRAINSY: What the hell you mean, my part?

DRIVER: Your part in the plan
>   To get this bird out of the bush
>   And right in my hand
>   <u>Before</u> the maskarade finish and be done!
>   The plan is this *(Confidentially.)*
>   Every night after rehearsals

61

I going to take me peadove with me
For a drive on Mayor Mitchell carriage
When the moon turn the sea
Into silver…
That is when the time will be ripe
And iron hot to strike…
All I want is a little time
To get her to
Turn her back on Cuffie
And come and live with me.

BRAINSY: How you going to get her to come to you?
What's the bait?

DRIVER: The landlord want his rent money.
She don't have any, nor the boyfriend!
For every drive she come for a drive
I put half the week rent money
In her hand,
Tell her I lend till after
The show she pay it back!
I lend her the first week rent last night!

BRAINSY: So is rent money you
Blind her eyes with?

DRIVER: Rent and romance…

BRAINSY: The boyfriend just going to stand by and
Let you romance off his woman?

DRIVER: That is where you come into the act!
We going to start rehearsal early.
Send off everybody else by nine-thirty
Then I will keep Quasheba back to practice
Her scene…

BRAINSY: And the boyfriend going to agree to that?

DRIVER: Use your brains. Ask the question.
What rumshops there for? And a friend?

Especially if I pay for the rum?

In advance.

So what's the plan?

BRAINSY: *(Slowly.)* The plan is that every night

When rehearsal finish early for everybody else

I must take off the boyfriend

To tour rumshop, pour

White rum down his throat

While you scamp off with his woman?

DRIVER: Go to the top of the class.

BRAINSY: Now you answer me one question

Why you think I going

To play the part you

Write for me?

You solve that problem!

DRIVER: Because this is the chance

You waiting for.

All these years.

The chance to open you hand

Spend money to dress the show

The way you really want!

To show this town

What you can really do!

To get the notice

People like us don't get

No matter how good we good!

To know what it feel like

Up there at the top.

For even one day! *(Pause.)*

Ah tired! Tired of

This second-hand life

That box me up with the Mayor Mitchell him

Day in, day out, shouting!

Drive here! Go there! Whoa!

You don't hear me say 'Stop', you black jackass!
And I, man, have to stand there
And take it!
Day in, day out!
And the Mrs Mitchell, she, with her stick!
Ruling the whole of us. *(Pause.)*
Driver, bring my medicine
This minute! Rat tat!
Maud, empty my chamberpot
Rat tat!
As if the whole earth
Is their own
The rest of us? Just cotch!

BRAINSY: For now. But a time will come…
Their rule will pass. Like Rome pass.
Then lowly people like you and me
Will find our chance at last.

DRIVER: We won't be here when it come.
The one life I have
Will be over and done…
So you got to understand, Brainsy man
When I see her, touch her
Like a force beyond me open the jail.
I no plaything of Mayor Mitchell then!
I'm what God make me for! I'm in command!
I have a universe of my own
Cut to my measure and fit.
And a part fit for a man to play in it. *(Pause.)*
Not no bargain basement role
Dress up in their coachman's clothes! Like this!

He flings the hat and gloves away violently. There is a pause.
He is embarrassed. The depth of his bitterness leaves a charge.
Change of tone as he struggles to gain control. BRAINSY signals to
DEAF-MUTE who brings DRIVER some rum and water. DRIVER

drinks. The music begins under. The 'business' gives time for a shift of mood.

DRIVER: That's why it's different

This time Brainsy…

DRIVER will sit and sing this part of his song, then get up for the more rhythmic second part.

DRIVER: *(Sings.)* This time it's real

Root deep I swear

This time it's real!

I feel a force

That's pulling me

I don't know where…

Up until this

I pledge I'd be

Devil may care…

Love here, love there

But love and leave

And who grieve, grieve!

So I never dream

The day would come

I'd feel a love that's leading me

I don't…know…where

And what's more

I don't care

And what's more

I don't care.

For I spy that peadove

High in the sky

She is my true love, my heart's desire.

Oh, I can't forget her

Don't care how I try,

I can't resist her

I'm all on fire! Fire! Fire!

So I'm out to win her

Cost what it cost
I'm out to get her
With no holds barred!

CHORUS joins in with back-up

DRIVER: The one fact I figure
This world belongs
To those who grab her
And force her hand!
Don't you let them fool you
'Bout the good reward
The good are losers
They end up last!
So I'm going to win her
Cost what it cost!
For I can't resist her!
I'm all on fire!
She's my heart's desire
I'm all on fire!
Fire! Fire! Fiyah! Fiyah!

CHORUS keeps up the 'Fiyah' until it dies away.

BRAINSY: Let me do some deduction
If I don't take part in the plan...

DRIVER: No money for costume.
Besides, we are friends.
Done?

BRAINSY: *(Hesitating, then as they shake hands.)* Done.

DRIVER puts on his top hat and gloves.

DRIVER: I have to run put the other
Part of the plan
Into operation.
I have to meet Quasheba and her boyfriend him at
Mayor Mitchell house.

He leaves.

BRAINSY: *(To DEAF-MUTE.)* You know, Deaf-Mute
I don't like it.

DEAF-MUTE looks back at him. Shakes his head. Doleful.

Alright, alright, so maybe
Driver making a fool of himself.
Young gal pull him down
Make him lose his sense…

DEAF-MUTE agrees enthusiastically.

And I know that it tough
For Miss Gatha and him
She don't have a child
And all that matter to her
Is Driver and Jonkunnu.

DEAF-MUTE agrees, miming 'Poor Miss Gatha'.

But what you expect me to do?
I am not God!
I only fool in Jonkunnu
Besides, Driver have a point, too.
A man got to feel
What it's like to be a winner
Even for one day in his life!
I can't get sentimental
About Miss Gatha and
Spoil my chance.
And yours too, Deaf-Mute
You going to get new costume
As houseboat.

DEAF-MUTE points to himself, delighted, leaps, twirls.

Yes, new costume for you too,
New costume for everybody!
More money for everybody all around!
A great great chance for me to

Dress this band as band never dress before!
Miss Gatha is Miss Gatha
But this chance is what matters! Agree.

DEAF-MUTE nods slowly to himself.

Deaf-Mute, me son!
On Christmas morning, 1841
On that morning I tell you one thing!
We going to shake this town!

DEAF-MUTE nods with enthusiasm.

We going to rock this town!
We going to rock this town!

DEAF-MUTE does a series of houseboat leaps, while BRAINSY moves down in position for his finale number, finale of Act 1. The CHORUS joins him downstage. As BRAINSY takes up his whip and drapes his old Pitchie Patchie costume about him, the CHORUS joins him as they sing and dance.

CHORUS: Dress! Dress! Dress!
Show! Show! Show!
Dress! Dress! Dress!
We're going to dress this show
And show this town
What they never see before
For it's our turn now
To call the tune
Our turn now
To lead the dance!
Our turn now
Our turn!

Blackout.

End of Act One.

Act 2

SCENE 1

Lights up on LOVEY and BOY. Their narration carries the pacing and briskness of last scene. They clap hands as they comment.

LOVEY: Chicken merry! Hawk is near!

Driver hunting peadove! Death hunting Driver!

People hunting Driver money!

BOY: New costume in Jonkunnu for everybody!

LOVEY: More pomp! More show! More pride!

More more money!

BOY: Reams of dreams, but some people dream the story one way...

LOVEY: And other people dream it different!

BOY: Different! Different!

LOVEY: Two people who everybody forget.

Two people who don't catch up

In the same dream net!

One is Miss Gatha!

BOY: And the other is Cuffie!

Driver forget one fact!

Cuffie is a Maroon!

And Maroon born for war! Ach!

The Ashanti-African dub begins here. LOVEY's style becomes more formal.

LOVEY: Now Maroon people come like the rest of us,

From another world called Africa,

From a different page that turn

Before the one we live now!

BOY: We can take that page as read.

Go on to Cuffie.

LOVEY: Cuffie's generation, long-time back
    Come from Ashanti-fighting stock!
    Different from the rest of us.

BOY: They catch and get sell
    Like the rest of us, Ashanti or not!

LOVEY: And passage the passage
    Across the sea that
    Salt like grief,
    Like the rest of us!

BOY: All that over and done with!
    Water under the bridge!

LOVEY: Water under the bridge for the rest of us.
    We settle for the little we can get
    And come to terms.

BOY: Only Maroon one hold out! Stubborn!

LOVEY: They have cause to stubborn!
    When they sail away from the old land
    They hide the Oxehead mask that dance the dead
    That dance the gods.
    They sail the mask on the sea with them!
    Carry the old power in the hold with them!

BOY: War Power!

Lights up on the Maroon version of the Maskarade. The ceremony will be like the one Bowditch describes. It features the Oxehead Mask, the mask of the ancestors. Its formality and gravity separate it from its cultural offspring, the Jonkunnu. War horns. Powerful drums. Dread. Colours of Earth. Colours, muted tones quite unlike the explosion of colour of the Jonkunnu itself.

War power!

Drums alone. Oxehead tied with rope, as he whirls. Sense of dread.

So hold your breath. Look away. Take care.
When the Oxehead dance in their masquerade
Is not man dance like you and me…

LOVEY: Is the gods!

Formal, short powerful dance, but muted. Formal drums. No other sound. Then it breaks off all at once. Mood and lighting back to everyday.

BOY: Driver forget one factor in the equation
Cuffie that meek young boy you see
Hanging round Quasheba
Love sick like puppy, not no stray dog,
Not no mongrel!

LOVEY: Cuffie trace his generation
Right back to
The warrior-chief John Konny that
Born and live in seventeen hundred…
And something.

BOY: Is his name give name to Jonkunnu?

LOVEY: Him same one. John Konny the self same
Ashanti chief that partner up with the Prussians
To fight off the Dutch, beat up the British!
He and the Prussians were in business.
Monkey business. Black flesh business!
Fighting and catching, buying and selling
Any black man that wasn't one
Of Konny's people!

BOY: *(Outraged.)* And it's his name
We celebrate
When we dance our maskarade?

LOVEY: Him same one!
In those days in the old land
One rule govern.
Inside the lineage, everything!

BOY: Outside the lineage…?

LOVEY: Tough!

BOY: So once the guns begin to flow…?

LOVEY: It was sell or be sold!
>Lineage fight lineage like the Dutch fight
>The British. The British fight the Prussians.
>Inside the nation everything.

BOY: Outside the nation?

LOVEY: Tough! The Prussians
>At the Dutch throat
>Till the day they sell out
>Their black flesh share
>To the Dutch, sell out
>Over Konny's head!
>The Dutch come with
>Their bill of sale!

BOY: Not a damn, Konny say!

LOVEY: The Dutch attack.

BOY: Single hand
>Seven long years
>Konny beat them back
>Seven years Dutch skulls
>Rattle in the dust
>At his gate
>Whisper his name *(Imitating a Dutch accent.)* 'Bevair! John
>Kanaus. Bevair!'

LOVEY: *(With nostalgia.)* Seven long years that
>Konny name noise up in the air!
>Black man sing of his fame!

BOY: But times change.

LOVEY: And like a great tree that the wind break
>Konny crash! Konny dead!
>*(Chanting. A lament.)* Konny crash! Konny dead!
>Konny dead oh!
>Like a great tree that
>The wind break!

    Konny crash and his people sell!
    Konny dead!

BOY: Konny dead?
    How Konny can dead
    When his lineage
    Carry his fame
    Across the saltwater of pain!

LOVEY: For they turn into a new lineage now
    The lineage of those who catch and sell
    The lineage of those who lose out!
    Their story turn to a different page now
    And freedom became the force now!

BOY: The force of Konny's name.

LOVEY: Konny men run away
    Join up with the Maroons.

BOY: The black slave runaways
    They call the wild ones
    The men that
    Whip can't tame
    Treadmill can't break.

LOVEY: The Maroons that set up
    Kingdom in the mountain
    Fight off the British!
    Beat them back, hunt
    Down the Redcoats!
    War after war!
    Till the British concede,
    Maroon free! Whilst
    Other black men still in chains
    Freedom was the force
    Of Maroon name!

BOY: But times change and
    Now like everybody else.

LOVEY: They pour into Kingston
    Doing another kind of hunting.
    Hunting work, hunting money
    Hunting fame – like Cuffie.

BOY: But work, money, job
    Or not, Cuffie stubborn!

LOVEY: Nothing else don't worth
    To him except
    The pride of his
    Maroon name.

BOY: And Maroon born for war! Ach!
    Born and bred.

Lights down on LOVEY and BOY. Up on MAYOR MITCHELL's front yard. MAUD is heard sweeping the yard off. CUFFIE and QUASHEBA are seated on the bench. They are eating from a cloth bundle that QUASHEBA has untied on the bench. Bread and fried fish. They are in a close mood. QUASHEBA brushes away some crumbs from CUFFIE's mouth with her hand.

CUFFIE: I dream a strange dream
    Last night…

QUASHEBA: What you dream?

CUFFIE: I dream I wake
    And it bright twelve o'clock
    Outside
    I hear you call my name
    But I can't see you nowhere
    I hear you say:
    The story over, Cuffie, I gone now
    You walk away.
    I see two shadow on the ground
    One is yours, the other is not mine.

QUASHEBA: But…

CUFFIE: I try to reach you

I can't move
I try to beg you
My mouth dumb!
I try to touch you
I can't find you.
I strike blind!
My life crash.

Sings. Reggae beat.

You are my man's dream
You are my pride
You are my reason to live or die.
You're sweeter than honey
And when my lips taste you
You tie up my heartstrings
You brand me for life!
So don't ever leave me
Don't turn your love from me
Don't let your eyes see
No one but me!
I won't ever leave you
Can't stop from loving you
Never there will for me
Be no one but you
No one but you!
So don't ever leave me
Don't turn your love from me
Don't let your eyes see
No one but me!

CUFFIE: Only one thing I want in my life
    For you and me to stay together like this!

QUASHEBA: That is my big dream too, Cuffie
    But there is another dream that I have
    On top of that
    A little dream…

CUFFIE: What dream is that?

QUASHEBA: *(She sits back on her heels. She has been stooping at the ground at his feet.)* To be Queen, Cuffie.

To be the Jonkunnu Queen
In the Kingston Maskarade make-believe *(Pause.)*
(Eager.) You will say yes then
Yes to the proposition?

CUFFIE: I will make up my mind
When the man come.
(He explodes.) And if the damn man don't come soon
I not even going to be here to say yes or no!
(He gets up, angry now, working himself into a fury.)
I am not a stray dog
For this man to keep me hanging
'Bout the yard where he work!
Who tell him that he can take any
Step with me? I not any mongrel!
When he come you can tell him
To take his Jonkunnu and stuff it!
I gone.

QUASHEBA: *(Firm.)* Don't bother to come back.
He returns threatening.

CUFFIE: What you mean?

QUASHEBA: What I say. If you don't say yes
We won't have anywhere for you
To come back to.
(They look at each other.) The rent we pay last week
Is the rent money
He advance me already.
This week rent due
This self-same evening…

MAUD enters, with broom. QUASHEBA breaks off. Turns to her.

QUASHEBA: What you think keeping

Mr Driver, ma'am?

MAUD: Nothing. Is so Driver stay.
He always late. By the way,
What's this I hear you tell
Miss Elizabeth
About you and Driver and Jonkunnu?

QUASHEBA: He ask Cuffie and me
To join our Jonkunnu band
And ask me to play Queen

MAUD: *(She stops what she is doing.)* You to play Queen?
You sure?
Driver want you to play Queen?

QUASHEBA: Yes ma'am.
And Cuffie to play Prince.

MAUD: Then tell me something.
If you play Queen
What happen to Agatha Franklin?

QUASHEBA: Agatha Franklin, ma'am?

MAUD: Yes. Agatha Franklin!
The best Jonkunnu Queen
In Kingston. And my long-time friend.

QUASHEBA: But Mr Driver...

MAUD: *(The penny begins to drop.)* He never tell you 'bout her?
He never tell you that
Agatha Franklin, the woman he live
With these past ten years
Is usual to play Queen in the band?

QUASHEBA: He only tell me ma'am
That he decide to get
A new Queen this year
Since the Queen they have
Not drawing the crowd any more.

MAUD: That's Driver alright!
>That's Driver kind of story
>Driver don't cut straight
>When he can cut crooked…
>Just wait till Gatha hear!

>*CUFFIE explodes on QUASHEBA.*

CUFFIE: You see what I tell you!
>The old man going push out the Agatha Franklin
>To make way for you
>Is you his eyes catch fire for.

QUASHEBA: Not so loud! Cuffie!

CUFFIE: What the hell you mean
>Not so loud?
>You don't see what I did tell you?
>You don't see what the old man up to?
>I want no part in this deal!

QUASHEBA: But the rent money, Cuffie?

CUFFIE: *(After a while.)* I have land, Quasheba
>Up in Portland mountain.
>We can go back
>I can plant yam
>You can reap and sell in the market.

QUASHEBA: That's what I come to Kingston
>To get away from.
>I have enough of that
>Hand to mouth life.
>I not going get old before my time
>Like my grandmother.
>You can go back to that.
>Not me.

CUFFIE: That life have something else
>Quasheba.

QUASHEBA: You tell me one

Thing that that
Bush life have
That I want?

CUFFIE: It have pride.
No man to tell you
What you can
Or can't do.

QUASHEBA: Times change
Maroon musket
And mountain bush land
Don't signify anymore.
You not different from anyone else.
You will have to change with it.

CUFFIE: And Maroon name,
Over three hundred years,
That don't mean anything anymore?

QUASHEBA: That name can't sell for a cent
In the Chinaman's shop…

CUFFIE: I never know
Life could back a man up
Against the wall, corner him
Like that.
Since we set foot in Kingston
Like I can't catch my life in my hand.
Can't even call back to my mind sometimes
What I was nor who I am.
Waiting here for that old man
For charity at his hand…
Taste in my mouth like gall.

QUASHEBA: I know. But as Grannie used to say
Hand in a lion's mouth, take time take it out
You have to stand on crooked to cut straight!
(Pause.) Besides you don't see, Cuffie?

If the old man have scheme
We can have scheme too.

CUFFIE: Scheme! Nothing but scheme!
Can't understand how
In this man's town
It's the self-same song:
Give, so you can get
Take all you can. Scheme for what you want
Not like where we come from
A man eat, his neighbour eat
That is the law that
Make man, man. *(Pause.)*
I not no stray dog
Scuffling for a day's work
From hand to hand.

QUASHEBA: But you don't see, Cuffie?
This is our chance now!
Our chance came round at last!
Once the Jonkunnu over and done with
We will have money to set up a little something
To make a little life for ourself, then
We can tell the old man to go dream his
Old man dream by himself!

CUFFIE: I can't do that!
I am a man.
Without pride a man is not a man!

QUASHEBA: Money is pride now, Cuffie.
Money pay the piper,
Money call the tune.
We have to go the way the world goes
We have to dance its dance!
But once the the play over and done
With money in our hand
We won't have to

Make believe nor form the fool!
It will be our turn then!
Our turn to call the tune
To lead the dance.

CHORUS: Our turn now to call the tune
Our turn now to lead the dance
With the money
In our hand
It will be our turn
Come at last!
Our turn to lead the dance
(Repeat throughout scene change.)

SCENE 2

BOY: Scheme upon scheme! And reams of dreams!
But some people dreaming one dream
And other people dream it different.

LOVEY: Chicken merry. Hawk is near.
For the one he should most remember.
Fire catch in Miss Gatha eye
When she hear the news
Like dry grass catch with tinder!

DRIVER and MISS GATHA's yard. MISS GATHA's Jonkunnu's Queen dress hangs on the line in the sun. She is seated in a rocking chair sewing on some of the beading that is loose. MISS GATHA is a tall, sombre woman. She is handsome. DRIVER enters with the tunic of his new costume over old trousers. He carries a swordstick. There is a piece of mirror stuck up over a box on which there is a basin. He begins to practice, trying to see how the tunic looks in the mirror as he moves. MISS GATHA looks at his tunic, looks down at the dress in her lap. Spot on LOVEY and BOY. The latter plays the tune of 'Fire in a Miss Gatha Eye' on the fife. A soft lighting also remains on GATHA and DRIVER. As BOY speaks GATHA begins to look steadily at DRIVER. The latter tries to appear nonchalant, as he lunges with the swordstick.

BOY: What a bitch when
    She begin to suspect
    The Dolly house mash up now!
    Her life with Driver
    Over and done with
    Throw away like scrapses
    On dry leaf fire!

Fade off BOY. Fife alone, soft under this scene. MISS GATHA shakes the folds out of the dress. She holds it up, looks at it. Quiet.

GATHA: Driver, look!

DRIVER: Look at what?
    You don't see I am practicing?

GATHA: I tell you, look!

DRIVER: Look at what?

GATHA gets up, goes to him. Holds up her dress besides his tunic.

GATHA: This? What kind of pappy-show
    You think I'm going to look beside you
    With the old satin frock yellow-up
    Besides your new costume!
    If you are going to make a jackass of yourself
    Playing Actor Boy at your age
    The least you can do is buy a new frock for the Queen.
    How you expect me to appear beside you in this?

DRIVER: You not going to beside me.

GATHA: What you mean?

DRIVER: You not playing Queen.

A long pause. She crosses to the rocking chair, drapes the dress on it.

GATHA: Since when?

DRIVER: Since now.

GATHA: Who say so?

DRIVER: I say so. Is my band. I decide. *(Pause. He begins to be uneasy as she stares at him.)* I make up my mind it's time for a change.

I find a new Queen!

GATHA: *(She goes up to him.)* A new Queen?

DRIVER moves away from her, goes over to the mirror stuck over the box with the basin, looks at his face, strokes his hair.

DRIVER: I ask a Jonkunnu band

To join up with me this year;

Bring fresh blood, excitement

Fresh face to

Coax more money out of people hand!

She goes up to him, touches his hair, looks at her fingers.

GATHA: *(Gentle.)* You been using Brainsy's bootblack

Black up your grey hair again

I well know what that mean. *(Pause.)*

So it's time for a change?

She must be young, eh, Driver?

So that the young can wash off

On your old age?

(Pause.) I can imagine how she feel!

How you excite her up

And full up her head

With dream *(Pause.)*

So you get yourself a new Queen

For the play?

And afterward?

For your bed and board?

DRIVER: What you think?

That I up to any funny business?

This is strictly business

Is not just the girl, I ask

Her boyfriend to play

Actor Boy Prince. How I could
Be up to anything
With her boyfriend in the play?

GATHA: A big part is a big bait.
(Silence.) So what part you decide
For me to play?

DRIVER: *(He gets up and goes inside. Brings out a large box.*
He opens it.) See it here. A brand new costume.
She says nothing. Does not even look at the costume.

DRIVER: You can help Pitchie Patchie
Collect the money
And share it out after.
Everybody know you honest.
That they can trust you
With the money.
What you looking like that for?
If men can play women
In Jonkunnu
Why women can't play men?
(Pause.) I make Brainsy buy
The best material for it.
Why you don't take it?

She takes the costume. But hangs it on the line without looking at it.
As she speaks DRIVER takes out the Executioner's costume and
hangs it on the line beside the Jack of the Green costume.

GATHA: *(After a pause.)* How life turn out different?
Different from what you expect?
(Pause.) Queen. Christmas morning
1830.
I was nineteen and ripe
As a poiciana
Flaming fire in the sun
Fresh and young.
No man hand touch me yet.

And pretty!
(Pause.) Agatha Franklin you pretty true
People would say!
I did think pretty
Was something that you just had
That would never end.

DRIVER: I did think so too.
That I would always
Go on
As I was.
That nothing would different.

GATHA: But you were the best looking man
I ever see!
I couldn't really believe it was me
You really want.

DRIVER: *(Overlapping.)* All that over and done with
It's best to forget.

GATHA: Driver Ransom wanted nobody else.
Same way it was for me too.
Don't care how the young men beg me.
On their knees!

She begins to get in the mood of her song. She becomes radiant in that past that is more real for her than the now.

GATHA: What a time that was!
All the men, every jack one
Begging and pleading
All the women, vex with me. Not one of them
Could hold a candle to me!
It was my time then!
I was the Queen of Hearts
I call the tune and centrestage,
I lead the dance!

This is her big number. She takes the stage over. She is no longer MISS GATHA whom life has frustrated but AGATHA FRANKLIN, Jonkunnu Queen, toast of the town. There is a kind of transfiguration in the actress playing the role. She is joined by DRIVER and the CHORUS as her dub begins. Sings.

GATHA: What a sensation! What a commotion!
    When I step out on the town
    In my Sunday frock
    With the train that sweep to the ground
    And the big bow at the back!
    What a carry go bring come!
    Oh, what a commotion!
    Who's that? People say,
    Who is that dressed to kill?

CHORUS: Agatha Franklin her name

GATHA: The word go round!

CHORUS: Agatha Franklin her name

GATHA: The name come round
    What a confusion! What a botheration!
    Not a man in the town
    Young man, old man, high man, low man
    That not in love with me!
    What a confusion
    Men just bowing, men just scraping
    Begging and pleading
    Falling all over their feet!
    All for the love of me!

CHORUS: Agatha Franklin is her name!

GATHA: Was the word on their lips!

CHORUS: Agatha Franklin her name!

GATHA: Was the dream that they dream
    With their eyes open wide
    Was the dream that they dream at night!

CHORUS (MEN): You should hear them sigh
    When she walk down the lane

CHORUS (WOMEN): You should hear them cry
    When she sweeps with her train

GATHA: How they beg me! How they plead!
    How they all want to marry to me!
    I give the same answer to all of them
    My heart I said was fancy free,
    (Spoken.) And I was out to keep it that way!

CHORUS: That's what she said!
    Till she meet her match!
    And Agatha Franklin free no more!

    Dance bridge.

GATHA & DRIVER: What a sensation, what a commotion
    When we stepped out on the town
    You in your Sunday frock
    You in your top hat and cravat
    With my train sweeping the ground
    As I tilted my hat!
    You should hear the carry go bring come
    All about the town!
    Match meet match! Yes sir!
    How the world go around
    Love meet love! Fire hot!
    Match meet match
    Oh, what a time that was

GATHA: I was the Queen of Hearts,
    And lead the Jonkunnu dance
    What a time that was…

    *DRIVER has turned away abruptly. GATHA only now noticing
    the change of mood, that he has broken out of the spell of the past
    in which she had caught him up, breaks off. A silence. She looks
    at him.*

GATHA: All that…over now…

DRIVER: Times change.

GATHA: I…can't change.

DRIVER: *(After a pause.)* Look, I have to go.

DRIVER goes, then turns.

DRIVER: If Slim pass by later
Give him the costume
For the Executioner.
Tell him to come to Brainsy's shop
Three nights from now
Dressed and ready for rehearsal.
(Casual.) And one other thing.
Since in your part
You only jump Jonkunnu
And collect the money
You don't have to come to rehearsal.
You hear me?

She looks at him.

DRIVER: Alright. Don't answer.
Do whatever the hell you want.
Just give Slim my message.
And for the little time
I have to remain here
Try not to look at me like that!
Your face so damn sour
It could curdle vinegar!

CHORUS: *(First time whispered. Second time sung soft and breathy.
'Fire' spoken on alternate beat throughout.)*
Fire in a Miss Gatha eye
Edo, edo.
Fire in a Miss Gatha eye
Edo, edo.
Send for the fire brigade

Put it out, edo, edo
Send for the fire brigade
Put it out, edo edo.

SCENE 3

The tune of 'Fire in a Miss Gatha's Eye' is played on the fife. A different mood.

LOVEY: *(Sombre.)* Fire flame, trap set!
Driver with his eye
Blinder than mine blind
Walking right into it.

BOY: Every night rehearsal dismiss
Early, early.

LOVEY: Only Quasheba Driver
Keep back, saying
They have to practise
In private!

BOY: Private! Private!

Drums begin to set mood.

LOVEY: Every night Cuffie
Eye blood red with fury
When Brainsy drag him off
To visit rumshop and Driver
Boldface

BOY: Tell him not to worry
For he will drive
Quasheba back!

LOVEY: The blood fly to Cuffie eye!
Driver feel the blood fly
Smell trouble draw at his back!
But all of a sudden

LOVEY: Driver don't care for nothing!

BOY: Don't give a damn

For God nor man!

LOVEY: For the old crook get
    Caught at last
    And meet his Waterloo.

Lights off. Up on BRAINSY's shop. DRIVER and QUASHEBA alone.

DRIVER: You light a spark in my heart, Quasheba.
    You blaze my body like bonfire
    I want to blaze like that
    For the rest of my life.
    Quasheba… *(He embraces her.)*

QUASHEBA: But…

DRIVER: No more buts. Make up your mind.
    Take your choice
    Young man without prospect
    Or old man with experience!

QUASHEBA: I can have a little time
    To think it over…?

DRIVER: Between now and tomorrow night.
    If you say yes, I put the world at your feet!
    If you say no, after the dress
    Rehearsal, Brainsy
    Can let down the new costume
    And Gatha can play Queen.
    She know the part in her sleep.

BRAINSY run in.

BRAINSY: Driver! Driver! Cuffie…

QUASHEBA: Cuffie!

BRAINSY: He give me the slip.

DRIVER: No problem. I was just leaving
    I have to pick up Mayor Mitchell
    At his girlfriend place.
    See you tomorrow.

DRIVER goes out. BRAINSY looks from one to the other, puzzled.

QUASHEBA: *(Calling after DRIVER, distraught.)* And I wouldn't
be Queen
Mr Driver?
You really mean that?

DRIVER: Remember Rule One of Teacher
Quasheba?
You can't get, if you don't give!

He leaves.

BRAINSY: *(Gently, he gives her his handkerchief.)* Don't pay Driver
any mind Quasheba.
Come, since we have the chance
Let me fit the sleeve of your costume
Come…

He gets a sleeve and begins to fit it on her hand.

QUASHEBA: You are a good man, Mr Brainsy.

BRAINSY: Not good Quasheba
But wise
Because I play the fool.
In Jonkunnu, in love, and in life!

QUASHEBA: The fool, Mr Brainsy?
He suddenly springs into his Pitchie Patchie role.

BRAINSY: *(Leaping.)* Dress! Make way!
For Pitchie Patchie
King of Clowns!
And Clown of Jonkunnu!
(Change of tone.) You see, Quasheba
Fool dream like other men
To wing a bird
That fly high in the sky.
But the fool know his reach.
The fool don't try
Instead

(He takes out the sleeve.) That length is fine Quasheba

You can go now

Good night…

QUASHEBA: What the fool do instead, Mr Brainsy?

BRAINSY: He take aim at his

High-flying dream

Mark. Aim. Fire! Shot! Drop!

And the fool laugh you see

Laugh at the dream that died!

Laughs at himself. Jonkunnu music held under.

QUASHEBA: *(Defiant. Transformed.)* My dream not to dead.

Mr Brainsy, I swear to God.

If it's the last thing I do

I am going to be Queen

In the Kingston of Jonkunnu!

When I step out on

Christmas morning people all

Up and down will say

'She's as good as Agatha Franklin.'

And some will whisper

'No, she's better.'

And some will shout it loud

She's the best Queen

Now, and forever!

I am going to be Queen

Of the Kingston Jonkunnu

Come hell or high water

Come flood or fire!

She whirls to see CUFFIE who has entered and is standing behind her. He looks at her, grimly.

QUASHEBA: *(Half pleading, half-defiant.)* For it will be our turn then

You don't see!

It will be our turn then
To lead the dance.

Still grim, he goes off. After a pause she runs after him.

CHORUS: Fire in Quasheba eye edoh, edoh
Fire in Quasheba eye edoh, edoh
Send for the fire brigade
Put it out edoh, edoh
Send for the fire brigade
Put it out edoh, edoh.

SCENE 4

Lights up on the previous setting. BRAINSY has brought the dummy centre stage. QUASHEBA's costume is fitted on the dummy. BRAINSY is kneeling in front, pinning up the hem.

BRAINSY: There now. I almost finish
I almost have it done.
(Pause.) Come flood or fire, eh!
Miss Quasheba?
(He looks up at the dummy.) So your dream not
Going to dead like mine?
Your dream not going dead?

He pulls the stool behind him, gets up from the kneeling position, takes a bottle of rum, pours a drink, drinks.

It wasn't true what
I say to you, you know Quasheba…

His theme song, i.e., 'The Fool's Song' begins to be played under with a beat which paces BRAINSY's speech.

I not wise at all!
Just a damn fool
Like every man else
Who light on you!
My eye catch fire
For you Quasheba

Catch fire with the best of them
Just like the rest of them
Driver, Cuffie
Only they can show it
Who going to believe that a Fool
Like me could dream
Of a girl like you.
A pitchie patchie fool
They would laugh you see.

Soft laughter from CHORUS. He pours another drink, gulps it down, prepares himself for his half-drunken song.

BRAINSY: *(Sings.)* I not going to cry!
When you say goodbye
I not going to cry

CHORUS: *(Laughing.)* He not going to cry!

BRAINSY: For true. And
I'll laugh in their eye
When they say
That I am the one in love with you.

CHORUS: In love with you? With who? He?

BRAINSY: I'll make sure to hide
What I feel inside
I'll make sure to hide

CHORUS: What he feels inside?

BRAINSY: What I feel for you
And I'll laugh in your eye
If you realize
I am the one in love with you!
(Rhythmically spoken.) What a Fool can do
Loving someone like you
Marking a bird that wing
High in the sky?
What can a Fool do

Aiming his heart at you
What can a Fool do
But let his dream die?

Lights off. Up on DRIVER's yard. MISS GATHA is seated in a rocking chair. MAUD, the servant has come to comfort GATHA but is uneasy in the face of GATHA's unresponsiveness. LOVEY and the BOY set the stage for what is to follow.

LOVEY: Reams of dreams

But everyone dream their dream different!

BOY: And a dream can dead

Just like me and you.

LOVEY: When a dream dead and smell to high heaven

BOY: Some take it make laugh, like Brainsy

LOVEY: Some take it make something else

Like Agatha Franklin!

MAUD fans herself with her headtie. She is nervous. GATHA's composure unsettles her, the latter's hauteur also unnerves her. The scene is played to a dub rhythm, so that the line between singing and speaking is erased. This gives it a formal 'blues' quality.

MAUD: *(As she fans herself.)* I did forget how far the walk far

From Mayor Mitchell to your
And Driver's yard. *(Pause.)*

GATHA gets up. Without a word, she pours water from a clay jar placed on a box under the tree. She brings the glass to MAUD. As the latter drinks, GATHA returns to her rocking.

MAUD: Is the Queen's frock that you have in your lap?

GATHA: Yes.

MAUD: You...going to rehearsal

This evening then?

GATHA: No.

MAUD: *(After a pause.)* I hear say plenty money spending

For new costume for Jonkunnu?

GATHA: Yes.

MAUD: A new Queen frock in it too?

GATHA: Not for me.

MAUD: *(After a pause.)* So you…know.

GATHA: Yes.

MAUD: That's what I did…

GATHA: Come to tell me?

MAUD: Yes.

GATHA: You could have saved yourself the trouble.

MAUD: It wasn't any trouble. *(Pause.)*

> After all is a long time
> Since you and me was friend. *(Pause.)*
> From we was children
> Playing game in the sun
> Besides when trouble
> Lick my life, left, right
> Up down
> Not always you
> To whom I turn? *(Pause.)*
> No trouble at all
> For me to come up here. *(Pause.)*
> I truly sorry for what I hear
> Gatha, I want you to know.

> *She gets up, comes closer to GATHA.*

> I know it hard, Gatha!
> We who feel it know it!
> But that is woman's lot
> So take time, take care!
> Just band your belly and bear! *(Pause.)*
> One day before you know it
> The whole thing pass!
> Over and done with.

One day you hear the name Driver
It don't even echo in your heart
One day come, you don't even
Remember who the damn man was:
You free, free at last.

GATHA: One day not now. *(Pause.)*

I desolate, Maud.

I desolate.

Pause. MAUD senses the depth of GATHA's mood, reacts angrily, quarrelling with the world, her usual defence mechanism, but with a great tenderness for GATHA.

MAUD: Driver going to pay!

For all that he do to you.

Driver make a bad mistake!

The day he join up with those Maroon

From Portland Mountain!

From the day I listen to that boy

Cuffie and watch him good

I say to myself, this time

Driver out of him depth!

Maroon people like that not

Like the rest of us. They deal

In heavy science and witchcraft! *(Pause.)*

(She whispers.) I hear say the Jonkunnu

They take out at Christmas

Not Christian. It African

From way back!

And in their maskarade

Is the dead and heathen god

That dance the mask.

Maroon people heathen.

Not like you and me.

They don't make joke!

Driver better watch out.

> *(Pause.)* As for the Quasheba she,
> Driver don't know what trouble
> He troubling when he push you out
> To make way for a scheming young
> Good for nothing like she!
> You of all people!
> The best Jonkunnu Queen
> In all of Kingston history!
> I don't know
> What the world is coming to!
> I vex you see! I vex!

GATHA: All that over and done with now
> All that make-believe puppet show.
> From now on the part I play is real!

MAUD: What you mean?

GATHA: Everything happen for a purpose
> Man only have to read the signs
> Then put his hand
> To do what he have to do!

MAUD: Gatha, take my advice. Let go of Driver.
> Put him out your heart
> Lock the door, dash away the key!
> Driver not worth it!
> The man fell on your life like a curse!
> All we other girl did know,
> Growing up with you, God
> Make you special! *(Pause.)*
> You don't know how I did proud
> That is me one you did select
> To be friend with. Maud miserable
> People say, have bad mouth and bad mind!
> Only you know there was
> More to Maud than that!
> More than quarrel and spite and curse!

Only you know what I have
To put up with, day in, day out!
With the three children
To feed and clothe
And not a man
To lend a hand.
Only you one know!
And you help me out
And not a soul know! *(Pause.)*
Yet still and all
I want you to know
The best gift you
Gift me with
Was when my eyes beheld
You step out as Agatha Franklin.
The best Queen
Of the maskarade show.
When I see you dance
The world open before me
Like a fan.
I pretty again and I fly
Like a kite in my hand!
Nothing in my life
Since and again
To match or beat
The way I feel
When I see you dance
The Jonkunnu Queen.
Whatever happen
I thank you Gatha
I thank you for it.

MAUD is crying silently. GATHA comes to her and wipes away her tears with the back of her hand. MAUD turns to go, then swings back. Quiet, but vehemently.

MAUD: So who dance or who won't dance

> Queen in this year Jonkunnu
>
> For me and other Kingston people
>
> There will never be another Queen like you!

She turns to go. She is weeping for the lost potentialities of their youth, the non-realization of their hopes. At the gate, she turns.

MAUD: Nothing! Before or since!

> As when you dance
>
> The Queen! Nothing!

MAUD goes quickly. GATHA has already forgotten her. As MAUD leaves, SLIM enters.

SLIM: Afternoon, Miss Maud, Miss Gatha!

> I am in haste
>
> You have the costume Driver leave here for me?
>
> But, by the way
>
> What this I hear
>
> About Queen?

GATHA: Yes.

SLIM: Then what part you playing then, Miss G?

GATHA: This year I write my own play, Slim

> This year I play my own part
>
> In my own scene.

Puzzled, SLIM watches as GATHA deliberately sits in the rocking chair, stroking the Queen's frock on her lap. As she rocks, she sings.

GATHA: Edoh, edoh, edoh oh

> Oh! Oh! Oh!
>
> Edoh, edoh…

CHORUS: *(Softly to beat.)* Man must pay

> What man owe
>
> That is the law
>
> The earth write down
>
> And what go up
>
> Must come down

To her ground!

GATHA: *(Sings.)* Sun hot bright outside
   And I am all alone.
   Sun hot bright outside
   And I am on my own.
   Edoh, edoh, oh, oh oh!
   Edoh, edoh! Oh…

CHORUS: For fire that light
   Must burn and burn
   Catch who it catch
   Hurt who it hurt!
   Fire that light
   Must burn and burn
   And only blood
   Can put it out!
   Only blood!

GATHA: *(Sombre, powerful.)* Edoh, edoh, edoh!
   Oh, oh oh!
   Edoh, edoh

   Blackout.

   End of Act Two.

Act Three

SCENE 1

Music: GATHA's 'Edoh' tune used, with drums reinforcing the 'edohs'. Then the fife or flute. This narration is more formal than the others. The pattern is that of a calypsonian like Chalkdust who uses the calypso form to put across complex ideas.

LOVEY: Now the other face appear!
    The face that hide behind our maskarade!
    The factor in the equation
    That everyone forget
    Is that life too have its hand in this affair!
    Life too have its plan and purpose, one
    That go far beyond their schemes and dreams
    Driver's, Cuffie's, Quasheba's.
    For the fact that Life keep back
    Like a wild card in the situation
    To play it like joker, come the time, come the
    Occasion
    Was the fact that Gatha
    Didn't dance Queen in Jonkunnu
    Dance it the best, like a woman possess
    Dance it all these years for nothing!
    The fact that Life keep back
    Was that when Gatha step her step
    One step forward, two steps back
    It's the Earth herself that dance that step.
    The Living Law that make man man
    That embody in her flesh! Rhythm
    It's commandment
    In the pattern of her step!

The BOY joins him, clapping rhythmically.

BOY: And as the rhythm step, the rhythm say:
    Share! Share my earth in common!
    Share food as you share my rain!
    Life's chance as you share my sun.

LOVEY: Or…I…the Earth
    Will wipe you out!

BOY: Now in ordinary time
    What the earth say?
    No sweat! In everyday time
    You look out for number one.
    Grab all you can? That's cool!
    Go on! As for you that rule,
    Ordinary time is YOUR time,
    Come on strong. Power enthrone!
    Hog up all of life's chances
    Wealth, woman, for you one!
    Who complain
    Thump them in their mouth!
    Lick every teeth down their throat!
    But wait until ordinary time done!

LOVEY: Wait until the edges
    Of the year have met
    When three hundred and sixty days
    Of ordinary time pass and gone.
    Then the time that mark
    By the wax and wane of the moon
    Appear at last!
    The five feast days
    That are out of time
    The holy days, the maskarade time.

BOY: Ordinary time reverse!
    Power uncrown! The king dethrone!
    Number one out for the count.
    The Queen Mother rule in.

> The rule reverse!
> The rule is share!
> The rule is love.

Jonkunnu music begins under.

LOVEY: All over the world,
   In Egypt at the festival of Zed
   With the river boat of Isis,
   In the Sumer of King Goudea
   In the New Year of China
   The Apo of the Ashanti
   The Purim of the Hebrew
   The Hussein of the Mohammedans
   The Mardi Gras of New Orleans
   The Incwala of the Swazis,
   The Calypso of Trinidad,
   The Maracatu
   From the Congo to Brazil.
   All over the world
   The rule is share
   The rule is love
   In the time that time reverse!

BOY: Laugh! All over the world
   The rule is laugh
   The fool enthrone
   As lord of all and give command:
   Break down all ranks,
   Bring all men to the ground
   Purge all hate! Remove all grudge
   Let love flow! And dance, dance
   To the rhythm of life's pattern!

LOVEY: Here is where, now is when
   Life trump with her ace.
   For since Life know
   That when Gatha step her step

In our maskarade play
Is the old Law that write
In the rhythm of her step,
Life plot it
So that the new Law
The Driver champion

BOY: That say 'take!'

LOVEY: Come into confrontation
With the old Law
That Gatha stake her claim on!

BOY: That say 'share'. Give back!

LOVEY: Or I the Earth will wipe you out!

BOY: *(Serious.)* That is the other face that hide
Behind our maskarade!

LOVEY: Let that other face appear!

BOY: Let the Jonkunnu come in!

LOVEY: Let the Maskarade begin!

Spot off LOVEY and BOY. Brilliant light on stage as the Maskarade troupe explodes onto the stage. Jonkunnu music under. PITCHIE PATCHIE dressed in a brilliant new costume, with a peaked cap, bells, and a whip, followed by JACK OF THE GREEN with a collecting bowl, and by the HOUSEBOAT and HORSEHEAD. They circle, PITCHIE PATCHIE using the whip to 'Dress back the crowd'. Since PITCHIE PATCHIE's opening speech is always topical it can be changed with each production to incorporate new and topical allusions. In a sense, very subtly, whilst the King and the Prince are the official heroes, the production must begin to build up PITCHIE PATCHIE since in the end it is he who will win the 'girl'. His style is as formalized as a clown or as a Calypsonian. Once again it must come clear that BRAINSY is the real 'artist' of the Band. In his role as PITCHIE PATCHIE he is transformed, a man come alive. He whirls and talks quickly.

PITCHIE PATCHIE: *(As he hits with the whip.)* Room,
Room, Kingstonians all

Please give us room we pray,
As we come to play our Maskarade
This merry Christmas Day!
In the year of our Lord, 1841

The HOUSEBOAT mask dances, leaping, whirling.

We are the best Jonkunnu band
That this town ever know.
In our Jonkunnu Houseboat
We carry good medicine
To purge the world
Of all greed
To let good feeling
Freely flow!
From you to me.
From me to you in return!
And on top of that
We offer good luck
At cut price!
Good luck for Christmas!
Success in the New Year!
Low prices, high wages
A pocket full of money
Cheap houses
Honest politicians
The negation of
Inflation
The Soviets out of Afghanistan
The Americans out of the Caribbean!
A dollar worth a dollar
A cent worth a cent
Peace on earth
Good will between men!
And in return for all this
Only a few cents

To meet our expense!

JACK OF THE GREEN goes round with the bowl.

Put a few cents in Jack of the Green's bowl
Times hard
Money small.

People on stage begin to throw cents etc. also from the audience.

Throw, throw
A comet up in the sky
Show that once and for all
This is world crisis
Or 'God's time'.
So take a break from disaster
Share a few cents
See our pleasant play
Let Lord Laugh drive away all hate
A few cents! That's it!

JACK OF THE GREEN busily collects as drums and fanfare.

BRAINSY: Now here begins our play:
Step in fair Queen. Clear the way!

QUASHEBA enters with her ladies. They step around the stage, dance the Jonkunnu step. She seats herself on throne.

BRAINSY: Enter bold King.

DRIVER enters, addresses audience.

KING: I am the king of courage bold
Who with his sword win a crown of gold
And with this fight win as my prize
Everything all at once:
House and land, kingdom and throne,
Rising stock dividends, taxes cut to the bone,
And you, the fairest of Jamaica's daughters!
View me, my Queen
My time is short

The criminal Warwick waits.
Wanting to rob me of this love
I have grabbed from life
To guard my age against the dark.

QUEEN: My Lord, my King, I beg you
Please not to leave me.

KING: I would not, love
But Death waits
Saddled and bridled outside my gate.
If fate's lottery should spin 'gainst me
Don't fret.
We will soon be together again
In an executive heaven
Where all the voters vote Republican
And stay the course with President Reagan.
Angels will police the streets,
Lock all losers out from destiny
And bar them from our lives.
Then you and me can live in peace, my Queen
With no more challengers to fight!
Then me and you can love, my Queen
In storybook style! Kiss me.

BRAINSY: Make way for the Grim Executioner!

KING: Executioner, these are my orders:
Keep your axe edge keen and bright,
Guard the Queen!
Kill all covetous knights
Whilst I fight the fight of my life.

BRAINSY: Kingstonians, clear the way!
Yonder come Warwick, the Prince.

CUFFIE enters with his accompaniment. Appropriate dances, etc.

PRINCE: Madame, my Queen and soon to be
My love

With the strength of this, my sword
And my right hand
As challenger
I stand before you now
A poor man of this land
Condemned to be, through no fault of my own
Out of work
And what is worse
Condemned to live without a destiny!
As a challenger I come to fight
For them who from the day they born
Lock out from life's chances.
In their name I stake my claim.
I hope to win love's fairest prize:
A crown and a throne; a job and a Toyota
And you ruling the kingdom of my heart!
And if I must tear this kingdom down
I will tear it to the ground
But I shall not lock out
From Life's chance ever again!

Shift of tone. He kneels.

I shall not lock out from love. *(Kisses her hand.)*
So I kiss your hand, my Queen.
I will return! Till then I beg
May your eyes not see anyone but me.

CUFFIE starts to go off to duel. Stops, then says:

Remember, Quasheba, what I tell you
Don't play me no play.
If he touch you up
And you don't push 'way him hand
As far as I concern, the play mash up.
You hear me?

EXECUTIONER/GATHA advances, lowering the axe. CUFFIE wheels away to the KING.

PRINCE: Guard your body
     Mind your head
     Watch how my sword will strike you dead!

They prepare for battle.

BRAINSY: Don't weep for them, my pretty love
     All men are fools.
     But I am a fool that knows I am a fool.
     And so, whilst they prepare to fight
     I'll take the chance to woo.
     They'll tell you it's for the love of you
     They draw their pretty swords
     It's no such thing, my love
     Power is what they want.
     The old one is afraid of death
     The young one afraid of life
     But I love you
     With the love of a fool,
     And the love of a fool is wise.
     The love of a fool will make you smile,
     Put laughter, like sunshine in your eyes.

Although BRAINSY as PITCHIE PATCHIE begins his wooing as part of the play, he should become quite earnest and convincing by now. It should be indicated that he really is falling in love with QUASHEBA.

QUEEN: You plead a cause that's all in vain,
     You offer sunshine for my love,
     But I sold my love for joy and pain
     And my love is not for sale again.

BRAINSY: Love as you will, love as you will.
     For what lose I?
     The folly of a foolish love
     The folly of a dream that died.

KING and PRINCE fight with their sticks using the movement of the Warwick stick dance, moving to the music. The crowd seethe with excitement and make encouraging comments. They fall silent as PITCHIE PATCHIE holds up his whip.

PITCHIE PATCHIE: One shall die,

One shall live

This is the challenge that we do give!

He brings down the whip and the KING and the PRINCE fight with their sticks using the movement of the Warwick stick dance, moving to the music. As they fight, lights on to LOVEY.

LOVEY: Couple sparks flying here and there,

But so far, so good.

The play still playing according to the pattern.

They fighting now

And just as it should turn out

The young prince supposed to win.

Touch the old king with his stick,

The old king fall down on the ground

Pretend him dead.

The Queen run to him

Call for a doctor to bring him back to life.

This is the pattern of the Maskarade Play

That did work out

When the Negro people

Take the pattern of

The Maroon Oxehead

And mix it in with

The Horsehead Festival

That the English people

Bring with them.

So in the play

In England as in Africa

A king dead

And a king resurrect;

Then all sing and dance
And shout hooray!
That is the pattern of the play.

Lights off LOVEY and BOY.

QUEEN: Oh woe is me! Oh woe is me!
My husband's dead and gone away
On the cold ground he's laid.

PRINCE: Now that he's dead
And his body is cold
We'll take him to the Church Yard
And bury him in the ground.

QUEEN: But the doctor has his part to play
In the Christmas Maskarade.
Tell the doctor to hurry come.
I'll pay any amount to bring my king back,
To love and life,
To save him from the cold, cold ground.
Where the doctor? Where? Where?
A doctor! A doctor! My kingdom for
A doctor.

*She runs distractedly up and down, peering into the crowd.
Everybody cranes to look, shading their eyes from the sun. Enter
BOY dressed in DOCTOR outfit. Mimes as in the traditional
Chinese Theatre manner, round and round the stage, urging on
an imaginary mule. Spot on him. He carries a hearing aid like
a tube and speaks in a loud voice as if deaf. The QUEEN is still
wringing her hands in an over-theatrical way.*

DOCTOR: Where's the patient? Show me him.

ONE OF THE CROWD: See the patient
Here, doctor
The patient is the king.

DOCTOR: A King, eh? That not going to be cheap.
Where's the patientee?

ONE OF THE CROWD: The patientee
　　Doctor? What you mean?

DOCTOR: How you mean what I mean?
　　The patientee? The person who is going
　　To pay me
　　My big fat fee.

QUEEN: I will pay you, doctor,
　　I am the Queen!
　　I will pay you anything, doctor, anything
　　If you can bring him back to me.

DOCTOR: Can? What you mean can?
　　I can cure a jackass who dead
　　For seven long years
　　What says a poor broken down
　　Rickety ramshackle King!

QUEEN: I know you can do it, doctor,
　　So do it for me.
　　You are well known
　　As the greatest doctor of medicine in this town.

DOCTOR: What you mean doctor of medicine?
　　Doctor of medicine come a penny a dozen.
　　I am a doctor of genetics!

QUEEN: What kind of doctor is that, sir?

DOCTOR: The only kind of doctor
　　Worth a cent!
　　Other doctors work to cure the sick body
　　Some even work to cure the sick economy
　　But I cure the body politic!

QUEEN: But what that have to do with
　　My dead husband, sir?

DOCTOR: What you want with that broken down
　　Old man you call you husband?
　　If it's a heir to the throne you want

Pay me $10,000

And I provide you with a test tube

Full of freeze-dry, freeze-fresh

Class A, genius sperm from my bank…

You want the millionaire model instead?

We have that too.

Take your pick! Which brand?

QUEEN: But doctor, it's my husband you came to revive!

DOCTOR: Cho! For $10,000 extra

I finish him off with an injection

So he never revive again.

Bring the cash. Give the word.

He takes out needle; prepares to make the injection.

QUEEN: But doctor, he's my husband!

And I love him!

DOCTOR: Love a loser! That's dysgenic!

QUEEN: Dysgenic or not, doctor

That is what write in the script

For me to say!

And it write in the script too

For you to revive him.

So that play have happy ending!

So you have to make him live!

DOCTOR: If you say so…

One pill called Instant Life,

One drink called Instant Growth,

A few drops of Development and Supply-side
Productivity.

Now, I put a drop on his temple, a drink in his throat,

A pill in his mouth. Pass a candle over him body.

Instant magic! Voodoo economics! You see?

He begin to move already!

KING groans, sits up, wipes his eyes.

KING: Where am I? In heaven? Or hell?

Or in love?

DOCTOR: Company, look on my good work:

I am a celebrated doctor of genetics

See how my instant magic works.

Rise up, you King. Join him, young Prince.

Come one, call all.

Join the dance of life lost

And life and love regained.

Come now, Mr Music Man,

Strike up the dance.

They all join in a circle. The KING with his arm round the QUEEN, the PRINCE on her other side. They dance with arms linked.

CUFFIE: Don't touch up my woman, I warn you!

Stop it. This minute.

Or I take this stick and break your head!

Not only the music, but everyone stops.

DRIVER: Which your woman?

She says yes to my proposition!

She is my woman now!

CUFFIE: Not a damn!

DRIVER: *(Putting his arm around her.)* Stop me.

Silence. CUFFIE springs at DRIVER with his stick, and they begin the stick fight. But this time not as a dance. At the moment when DRIVER hits away CUFFIE's stick, leaving him defenceless, everything freezes. Lights on to LOVEY.

LOVEY: Driver hit away Cuffie stick now?

BOY: Yes, sir.

We see the actions as a gestural mime as LOVEY questions the BOY.

LOVEY: Driver forget himself now

Turn the sharp end of the stick,

Run it right into Cuffie…?

BOY: *(Hushed.)* Yes, sir.

LOVEY: Driver come back to himself now
Realize what he do
Draw back…?

BOY: Yes, sir.

LOVEY: Ah.

> *CUFFIE has fallen to his knees, his hands clutching at the stick, pulling it out. The Executioner moves forward, stamps the long-handled axe on the ground before CUFFIE, who draws himself up on the axe, swings it high above DRIVER, brings it down, as DRIVER reaches for CUFFIE's throat. The axe comes down. They fall dead together. Silence.*

LOVEY: The two of them, King and Prince
Slide over the edge of the light
And into the dark.
Two Actor-Boys, stone cold dead
On the cold ground.
Christmas, 1841.
Dead, stone cold dead.

> *Silence. The BOY, awed, moves away from LOVEY. He recounts the next events in a voice something like that of a radio commentator, but he whispers so as not to break the mood. The KNIGHTS take their sticks to each other in the dance fight, and the BOY's narration is done to the clicks of their sticks. The lighting on the KNIGHTS is dim, so that the focus is on the BOY.*

BOY: Then the Knights of Driver
Take them stick to Cuffie's Knights
And Cuffie's Knights lick them back.
The fight spread like contagion
To every Jonkunnu band in Kingston.
It was war all right!
Mayor Mitchell vex out of him mind
Declare Jonkunnu abolish.
Kingston people blood up

Riot bruk!

Soldier pour into Kingston town.

Scarlet coat, fire and smoke

Blood! All around.

Till under the shadow of the gun

Kingston grow quiet.

Under the prow of the cannon

Kingston stay quiet!

As DEAF-MUTE places the axe in the basket, BRAINSY goes up to the EXECUTIONER, spins him round to face him.

BRAINSY: Alright, Slim!

So you give the boy the axe

What the hell you think?

GATHA: Not Slim.

BRAINSY: So Slim?

GATHA: Play the part of Jack of the Green

BRAINSY: And you?

GATHA: I do what had to.

Must and bound.

Measure that deal out

Must deal back in return.

BRAINSY: But…

GATHA: I write a different end

To a different play.

GATHA moves over to where QUASHEBA sits on her knees. GATHA gazes at the feathered headdresses, picks up the King's headdress, then puts it back. She takes off the Executioner's robe. She leaves. BRAINSY begins to fold the robe carefully. DEAF-MUTE has picked up everything else except the two headdress masks. QUASHEBA continues to hold onto them and says to DEAF-MUTE, as if trying to convince herself.

QUASHEBA: I did love Cuffie, you know

I did love him bad.

I didn't feel anything for the old man at all.
Cuffie didn't believe me
But I didn't feel a thing.
It was only the rent money he was going to
Give me.

Not hearing her, not noting her, DEAF-MUTE relentlessly draws away the headdresses.

Why I was going with him
For a drive, in a carriage by the sea.
Sweet like a dream
In the silent silver kingdom of the sea.

BRAINSY comes over.

BRAINSY: But the play over now.
Come.

QUASHEBA: But the dream dead, Mr Brainsy!
You don't see!
What left for me to do now?

BRAINSY: Come home…with me.

QUASHEBA: You…?

BRAINSY: With the Fool.

QUASHEBA hesitates.

The dream have to make over
Now. Again.
You don't see? *(Pause.)*
Who left to do it?
But we ourself… Come!

BRAINSY helps her up, taking the feathered headdresses of the King and Prince from her. They exit. Lights back on LOVEY and BOY.

LOVEY: So, the one we least expect
The Fool gets the girl.

BOY: *(Interrupting.)* So this is where Life's plot come in!

He begins to rise, more and more carried away by the excitement of his discovery.

This is what Life did see
That the time of the Prince
And the King, of the sword
And the gun, of the fairy story
That all's well that's lost for love
For honour, glory, and even money
That that page over and done.

LOVEY: *(Approving.)* Now…you initiate!

BOY: *(Still working out his discovery.)* And the time of the Fool
Who make life worthwhile to live
For every woman, man, and chile.
Who laugh away the old tales
That tell say
That those on high who box in
Lowly people's chance to realize
The bright and dazzling in our lives
Do so by right!
And the time of the Fool
Who cut that right
Down to size
With the weapon of his smile.
Who retell the old tales
So as to change in men's hearts
The feel of what is right!
(Pause.) Who reverse ordinary time
To maskarade time
With the laugh that he laugh
In the sun! *(Pause, wondering.)*
That time…the time of the Fool…
Me! Has come!

LOVEY: *(Handing the BOY the necklace that is the insignia of his trade.)* Here…you graduate

So take the tools of your trade.

BOY: I…am…?

LOVEY: You license now

You are a full-grown spinner of dreams.

A Master teller of tales.

BOY leaps into the air with a great shout, then suddenly remembers. Concerned.

BOY: But you?…

LOVEY: I pass on to you

The tale that pass on to me.

It's your turn now

To turn the new page

To sing the strange, the new

The different verse! My task is done.

Pause. As it sinks in, the BOY gives a great leap. The finale music begins under the BOY and CHORUS as they chant and dance to the rhythm of the music.

BOY: Jonkunnu play over?

Jonkunnu play just begun!

And it's my turn now

To carry on

The maskarade that first began

In Africa with

The birth of man!

Before the Sahara

Turn to desert sand!

Long before Sumer, Egypt, or China!

Long before Genesis or Greece!

So let the dream spin again

And let the tale retell.

Till we reinvent

A lineage

New, of man!

Till we reinvent the first invent
That we invent!

CHORUS: Ourself!

BOY: So let the dream spin again
Let the tale retell
Till we all know who we are
Till we all know
Where we are from.
We're the lineage of the stars
And the universe is ours.
We are of high royal estate
And shall not know
Want or pain!
Ever again!

CHORUS: Never! Ever! Again!
So we are serving notice now
We shall take this old world up
We shall turn it upside down
And remake it as our own!
And no one shall ever know
Want or pain! Ever again!

BOY: So let the dream spin again
Let the tale retell.
Let us rhythm to the pattern
That the Earth has set!
Let us dance clan by clan
In the maskarade of man!

CHORUS: The maskarade of man!

BOY: For we shall dance
Clan by clan

CHORUS: Yet all as one

BOY: So that the maskarade of man
Will go on!

CHORUS: Go on!

BOY: Maskarade play over?

CHORUS: Maskarade play just begun!

Everyone in the cast dances.

The End.

Notes to Maskarade

- The spelling of *Maskarade* is intentional. The playwright wishes to convey the cadences of the Jamaican pronunciation of masquerade.

- An early version of *Maskarade* appeared in a 1979 Jamaica Information Service 'West Indian Plays for Schools' booklet, volume 11, edited by Jeanne Wilson.

- A screenplay by Lloyd Reckord exists: *Queen of Jonkunnu* based on the stage play *Maskarade,* music by Harold Butler, lyrics by Jim Nelson, book by Sylvia Wynter (© 1990. Reckord Films).

Appendix:

The Jonkonnu Festival: What exactly is Jonkunnu as practised in Jamaica?

- **Cheryl Ryman**: 'Jonkonnu masquerade bursts forth from the pages of history as the earliest traditional dance form of African descent still to be found in Jamaica.'[1]

'Simply put Jonkunnu is traditional street festival based on age old rituals brought with the African slave on his Middle passage. It takes place at Christmas time. Several members of a troupe elaborately, often frighteningly costumed as traditional characters such as Cow Head, Horsehead, Pitchie Patchie, King, Queen, Bellywoman, The Devil, Houseboat amongst others use dance, mime, gestures and masks harking back to memories of an African homeland and culture to enrich the ritual and heighten the effect. This festival, once widely popular in Jamaica, currently takes place on a much reduced scale, amidst a culture rife with centuries of racial exploitation. In the parade (or performance) music, (usually from drum and fife), is an essential element. One enduring object of the Parade is to elicit donations from an appreciative crowd of onlookers…'.

Sylvia Wynter's paper 'Jonkunnu in Jamaica: Towards the interpretation of Folk Dance as a Cultural Process', which was published in part in the *Jamaica Journal* Vol. 4.2 in 1970 and is a detailed consideration of Jonkunnu is too lengthy to include the entire text here. However below is a selection of excerpts from this paper to aid appreciation.

'The Jonkonnu or John Canoe festival had its beginning in a cultural process that (Hans) Sloane[2] witnessed and described in the seventeenth century.

The rise of sugar on the world market made Jamaica a sugar society. Each Estate was an enclosed world and although the refusal of the Jamaican planters to Christianize their slaves (…)

---

1   *Jamaica Journal* February 1984, Vol 17, No 1: 'Jonkonnu: A Neo-African Form' by Cheryl Ryman.

2   **Hans Sloane**: A voyage to the islands Madera, Barbados, Nieves, St Christophers and Jamaica privately printed in 1725.

prevented the later acculturation that would take place, there were points of contact between the English, Scotch and Irish indentured servants, and particularly the bookkeeper class. It was through this class, poor, cut off from much contact with their fellow-whites, living in concubinage with African, creole, and mulatto women, that some sort of cultural fusion must have occurred.

The Morris dance is part of the spring festival, where young men dance for the renewal and continuance of life. It is, in effect, 'medicine dance' handed down through the European counterpart of the secret societies 'which practised the medicine religions that conditioned life in Europe before Christendom'... Each Morris group had a leader. There were several characters who made up the group. The hobbyhorse, which became the Jamaican horsehead was only one of several animal men. The dance distils the medicine 'in rhythmic waves which reach the trees and animals and houses and people, quickening to life, washing them clean and making them whole. Another type of Morris dance, the horn dance, was a fertility medicine dance. Apart from the spring rites, there were mid-winter rites. It is in these rites that we find the 'Sword dance-cum-Play' which was to become one aspect of the Jonkonnu. Like the Morris Dancers the swordsmen are seen as actors 'who once disguised themselves, blacking their faces or covering them with masks'. They, too, had the same retinue of characters: hobbyhorse, clown, the woman, a Dirty Bet, of sometimes a king or queen, lord or lady and often a quack doctor, and his man Jack.

The Egungun secret society of the Yoruba is a cult... An Egungun, which is, in effect, a Jonkonnu as mask, dancer and leader of the group, is seen as the embodiment of the spirit of a deceased ancestor who returns from heaven to visit his people. The word *Egungun* itself means 'masquerador'; in the Jonkonnu celebration described in 1925 the group referred to themselves as 'masquerradors', rather than Jonkonnu...

The Mask, i.e. the costume, must entirely cover the dancer. He carries a whip and speaks in a ventriloquial voice.

From Long's[3] description, the sword is in his hand, rather than the whip – and the fact that the dancer bellows out as he dances 'John Connu' – may suggest the influence of the English Sword-dance-cum-Play

The plays, like the English folk doctor-play had the power of transformation of reality. There is a fusion of procession and doctor-or-cucumby's play, which makes it an interesting parallel with the Jonkonnu, as writers after Long described it. The death and rebirth 'doctor-play' features as part of Jonkonnu by 1801 when Lady Nugent described it. 'On Christmas Day', she writes, 'the whole town bore the appearance of a masquerade'. There are many 'Johnny Canoes' and many 'strange processions' and groups, made up of 'dancing men and women'. Apart from the processions, 'there was a party of actors. Then a little child was introduced...a king who stabbed all the rest...some of the children...were to represent Tippoo Saib's children and the man was Henry IV of France. After the tragedy they all began dancing with the greatest glee... The tragedy was the 'doctor-play' mock duel at the end....'

It is obvious from these descriptions that the version of the Sword-Dance-Play that had become popular in the Jamaican Jonkonnu was the version with the duel at the end, in which the two protagonists fight with swords; one is killed, but, revived by the music, gets up and dances – whether a sword dance between the two contenders, or a general dance. Excerpts from Shakespeare and other plays were then performed, but according to Belisario[4] – whose sketches and descriptions of Jonkonnu are invaluable – these excerpts were all fitted into the pattern of the folk play: their ending kept the same ritual and significance.

Whatever might have been their performance, says Belisario 'Combat and Death invariably ensued, when a ludicrous contrast

---

3   **Edward Long** (August 23, 1734-March 13, 1813) was a British colonial administrator and historian, and author of an influential work, *The History of Jamaica* (1774).

4   **Isaac Mendes Belisario** (1794-1749) born Kingston Jamaica, educated in England where at the age of 18 he had already exhibited at the Royal Academy. He returned to Jamaica in 1834 at the age of 40 and by 1837 his Sketches of Character were complete:. These 12 sketches were hand-drawn hand-tinted lithographs of five rural Jamaican landscapes and seven Jonkunnu characters.

was produced between the smiling Mask and the actions of the dying man. At this Tragical point there was always a general call for music – and dancing immediately commenced – and this proved too great a provocation usually to be resisted even by the slain, and he accordingly became resuscitated and joined the merry throng.'

Belisario tells us that the concept of the competing sets and Set-Girls was brought to Jamaica from Haiti by the French refugees and their slaves and servants who accompanied them when the Haitian War of Independence began. In Haiti, the French Catholic Carnival, itself a rite similar in some concepts to the Jonkonnu, with pagan elements reinterpreted in Christian-Catholic terms, set the dominant patterns; but already infiltrated by African elements, such as the use of drums and rattle.

Through the French Set-Girls, the Creoles (i.e. Negroes born in Jamaica) began to dominate the Carnival. The Jonkonnus were still part of what Chambre terms the 'Johny Canoeing' on the north side of the island, which was a 'splendid affair' but they were a subsidiary part in Lewis' account; and even the costume of the Jonkonnu chief masked dancer was creolized in some aspects. 'Monk' Lewis describes the Jonkonnu chief dancer as 'a Merry Andrew dressed up in a striped doublet and bearing on his head a kind of pasteboard houseboat filled with puppets, representing some sailors, others soldiers, others again shown at work on a plantation.' Lewis was one of the earliest writers to describe this 'houseboat' mask.

From Belisario's sketches and descriptions of the Jonkonnu band, just before the festival in its more elaborate form disintegrated, it is obvious that the houseboat mask was a very special mask for the leader. The mask of the other characters such as COW HEAD, and HORSEHEAD were animal masks borrowed from the African and the English folk ritual. The mask of KOO-KOO or ACTOR BOY, while elaborate, does not seem to have any particular symbolism... The name KOO-KOO which has given rise to a most ingenious explanation recorded by Belisario, nevertheless seems most likely to derive from the Yoruba word – KU, which means 'a luminous spirit', i.e. that which a good man becomes after death. The word IKOKO, related to the same root refers to the food, drink and meat offerings that are put on the graves in pots. This food is supposed to belong to the *Kas* or spirits of the dead. KOO-KOO is most likely related to both these words, since the Egungun cult was an ancestral cult; and in this context ACTOR BOY would embody the ancestral spirit. His pantomimic gestures in the Jonkonnu procession which seemed to refer to his hunger, would perhaps be intended to remind that the 'spirit' must be fed; and perhaps by implication that the group must be rewarded with good tips.

ACTOR BOY, Belisario also tells us, some ten years before (i.e. before 1837) played one of the main parts in the COMBAT-till-Death version of the doctor plays. He most probably played the part of the younger protagonist who gets killed, is restored to life, and joins in the dancing. But the creolized version of the Jonkonnu began to lose much of its original meaning, and by Belisario's time, ACTOR BOYS were 'reduced to displaying their finery' and 'to the performance of certain unmeaning pantomimic actions'. The significance of most of the other characters sketched by Belisario had also become confused. Yet a character like Jack-in-the-Green who stands with the Set-Girls in one sketch, carried religious connotations in both his English and his African meaning.

The Jonkonnu houseboat also carried religious connotations, as both Williams and Chambre indicate. The Horned mask, the Oxhead mask and its symbolism was clear. Why did this mask give way to the houseboat? Did the Jonkonnu figure sketched by Belisario, in 'mask, wig and military jacket, posing upon his head the house-shaped cap glittering with mirrors and tinsel and topped by a tufted dome or peak' still carry a religious connotation, in spite of his secular and European-type dress? Was the houseboat an African mask in an original form? Or has an old artistic form and function – the mask – been translated to the New World to create a new mask for a new reality?'

Playwright's notes:

The characters Driver and Maud. Driver's split personality, Act 1, scene 4 (p40). This scene reveals the two sides of Driver. He reveals his real bitterness, his sense of entrapment in a secondhand life, his bitterness at his employers and the dominant middle-class white world which 'down-presses' him. Not giving him a chance to realise his potential. Thus his theme song is in two parts: (a) the Introduction which is more intimate and lyrical but with the ska-reggae beat that will explode in the second part; (b) the second part of the song will suggest that like Guede, one of the Odun Gods, he is moral, a life force whose ethic is his vitality and force-force in the biological and African ontological sense. Like John Konny, he is, from the Judeo-Christian perspective, ethically ambivalent.

Maud's ambivalence towards Gatha. Maud has a contradictory relationship with Gatha. She likes her, but feels that she is in strange territory with her, respects her, but resents the way in which Gatha keeps herself to herself, asking no quarter from anyone, compelling respect, remaining apart from the others. She pities Gatha on the other hand and identifies with her. We see her here (in Act 2) out of her servant role, the role imposed on her by the social order.

The setting for the play:

The set must catch the opposition of the Blue Mountains, the plains and the sea. The two-level stage serves to mark the difference – interaction of past and present. When the play begins the Jonkunnu Festival has had to take refuge in the hills; to go underground like the Maroons. The sense of an underground existence needs to be brought out.

Alternative Cuffie song Act 2, Sc. 1

You are my man's dream
You are my pride
You are my reason to live or die.
You're sweeter than honey
Your lips seal the taste
You tie up my heartstring
You brand me for life!

Bridge:

So don't ever leave me
Don't take your love from me
Don't let my eyes blind
Don't cut my heart strings
Mash up my pride
For if I should lose you
I'd strike blind!

The Jamaican Maroons:

The escape into the mountainous interior of the island by (some of the) slaves – especially the Kromanti – who were to become famous as the Maroons, began early under the Spaniards. The Maroons humanized their mountainous interior with adaptations of their own culture.

(In 1739-40 the British governor in Jamaica signed a treaty with the Maroons in which they were granted 2500 acres of land in two parishes of the island Portland and Trelawny. The single female National Hero of Jamaica is Nanny (?-1733), a Maroon warrior Queen who waged successful war on the British.)

Editor's notes:

DUB:

Dub is the recording engineers' art of deconstruction where a reggae composition is stripped down to its drum and bass skeletal structure and reconfigured, recreated with fragments of other instruments, enhancing the danceability of the music. Linton Kwesi Johnson: *Writing Reggae: Poetry, Politics and Popular Culture Jamaica Journal,* Vol 33, Nos 1-2.

TOPICALITIES (Anachronistic references)

Maskarade records events in 1841. It is highly unlikely that black peasants jumping Jonkunnu in the streets of Kingston would refer in jest to the political landscape of the United States of America in 1983: e.g.

Now some people might think, say/That the tale we going to tell/Just a nice little piece of 'ethnic' business! /So let me warn you from the beginning/I'm not no folklore Uncle Remus/With a fake lore masquerade/For some of you to come and get/Your doctorate on.

Or as Brainsy says:

And the clip clop and the luxury of the carriage/Work the trick!/ Tricknology! You have/Your doctorate in it!

Pitchie Patchie desires: Low prices, high wages/A pocket full of money/ Cheap houses/Honest politicians/The negation of/ Inflation/The Soviets out of Afghanistan/The Americans out of the Caribbean!

And the King admits to his worry about rising stock dividends and taxes cut to the bone but promises his love they will soon be together again in an executive heaven where all the voters vote Republican and stay the course with President Reagan. The doctor, a qualified geneticist who offers test tube designer babies through his freeze-dry class genius sperm bank, prescribes pills called instant life, a few drops of development and supply: Instant Magic: Voodoo Economics.

Thus, *Maskarade* employs a well-established Jamaican theatrical tradition which flourished in the annual local pantomimes where the lead actors would engage in unscripted 'front of curtain' dialogue/banter commenting on the news/scandals of the day while successfully masking the changing of the scenes behind the curtain. These dialogues were called Topicalities. As this version of the play was performed for University audiences in the United States of America, the playwright has used 'Topicalities' which would amuse and have relevance for her audience.

Jamaican dialect:
Maugre: very thin, underfed.
(Page 42, Maud, 1ˢᵗ speech, line 8)

Johncrow: local name for a vulture.
(Page 44, Quasheba, penultimate line)

Old higue: a miserable cantankerous woman.
(Page 46, Elizabeth Jane, line 19)

BEDWARD

A PLAY IN TWO ACTS

BY LOUIS MARRIOTT

Charcoal portrait of Alexander Bedward
by Ray Jackson

BIOGRAPHY

Louis Marriott (1935-) is a Jamaican playwright with over twenty plays for theatre to his credit including the classic *Pack of Jokers*, *Playboy* and *Bedward*. He has written scores of programmes for radio and television including the University of Brixton for BBC radio. Apart from having been Deputy Editor of Publications for the Commonwealth Parliamentary Association and Editor of *Public Opinion*, his journalism has been syndicated in some 200 English-language newspapers and magazines throughout the world. He has been a regular guest writer in several Jamaican newspaper publications. Having held several posts in Senior Public Relations including that of Government Public Relations Officer and Press Officer for Jamaican Prime Minister Michael Manley, he is currently the Executive Officer of the Michael Manley Foundation, a member of the Performing Rights Society and the Jamaica Federation of Musicians.

Performance History

The Shepherd (Initial title)	1960 at the Ward Theatre, Kingston Jamaica
Bedward	1984 at the Little Theatre, Kingston Jamaica
Bedward	1993 at the Ward Theatre
Bedward	2012 at the Karl Hendrickson Auditorium, Kingston Jamaica

Cast of the original 1960 production of *The Shepherd** (in order of appearance):

Shakespeare Woods	Derek Boughton
Ruth	Myrtle Robinson
Sarah	Inez Hibbert
A Man	Karl Binger
Bedward	Charles Hyatt
Dawson	Winston Tate
Colon Man	Vernon Estick
Inspector	Raymond Jackson
Visitors to Stream	Percival Darby, Orford St John, Raymond Mair, Herbert Marriott, David Ebanks
Roman Henry	Philip Harry
Steele	Trevor Rhone
Sergeants Major	Robert Dixon
	David Lindo
A Woman	Joyce Walker
Census Enumerator	Audley Butler
Jabez Plunkett	Adolph Silvera
Corporal	Fitz Weir

Chorus   Louise Alberga, Winnifred Anderson, Valda Arbouin, Verona Ashman, Edna Baker, Barbara Beavers, Sidney Beckles, Elaine Brown, Olive Brown, Henry Bryan, Millicent Clarke, Wolsey Cornwall, Grace Davis, Pearl Dickenson, Neville Downie, Michael Hanson, Mae Headlam, Mae Holder,

Winnifred Logan, Daphney Mahoney, Delford Malcolm, Dudley Marriott, Ludlow Marriott, Mickie McGowan, Monica McGowan, Eva McLarty, Pam Morris, Gloria Mullings, Clem Patterson, Rex Rose, Billy Scott, Una Sheldon, Egerton Sinclair, Dorothy Smith, Daphne Walsh, Elaine Walsh, Audrey Wood

*The play was then called *The Shepherd* and was later changed to *Bedward*.

The cast of the 2012 performance at The Karl Hendrickson Auditorium, Kingston, Jamaica (first perfored: March 3, 2012):

ALWYN SCOTT	Bedward
BARBARA MCCALLA	Mrs Bedward
WINSTON 'BELLO' BELL	Roman Henry
GRACE MCDONALD	Sarah Plunkett
MICHAEL FORREST	Inspector
TEDDY PRICE	Shakespeare Woods, Sergeant Major
TREVOR FEARON	Dawson, Enumerator, Dr John Edwards
JEAN-PAUL MENOU	Governor, Reporter, Government Chemist
MAURICE BRYAN	Steele, Sam Burke
RENEE RATTRAY	River Muma, Chorus
HUGH DOUSE	Guard, Jabez
TOMEKHA MCCARTHY	Pumpkin Woman, Chorus
DAMION CAMPBELL	Chorus
CHRISTINE POWELL	Chorus
DANIELLE WATSON	Chorus

Directed by Yvonne Brewster

Designer Ron Steger

Musical Director Noel Dexter

Movement Consultant Maria Smith

Lighting Designer Nadia Roxburgh

Stage Manager Alvin Campbell

ASM Pamella Bennett

Introduction to *Bedward*

by Louis Marriott

I was born in May 1935 into a Jamaican family steeped in arts and crafts and public affairs.

My paternal grandfather was an all-round craftsman who moved his family to the north coast to sell craft items to the first wave of tourists visiting Jamaica.

Earlier, grandmother Marriott operated a crude outdoor theatre at their home in a village on a hill overlooking the city of Kingston. An amateur playwright, producer, director and musician, she presented original works – mostly musicals – on a mound stage. Her audience sat on bamboo benches implanted in a hillock that sloped down toward the stage. Her cast comprised family members, neighbours and friends.

My father, as a young master carpenter and jack of all trades, migrated to Kingston; married; established himself as an amateur playwright, producer, director, actor, singer and guitarist; built a backyard theatre; sired nine children; and peopled his stage with family members, neighbours and friends.

When I made my debut as an actor at age two, in early 1938, Jamaica was entering into its final stage of decolonisation. Later that year, my father signed up as the 109th member of the political party that would spearhead the campaigns for universal adult suffrage and self-government.

Whereas his mother's theatrical works raised funds for her church and local charities, our beneficiaries were the nascent political movement and the Universal Negro Improvement Association (UNIA) of Jamaica's global black liberator, Marcus Garvey, although we were not Garveyites. Understandably, the theatre in which I was initiated was indigenous, largely heritage-based and satirical.

In January 1947 I entered an elite boarding high school by the only available route, a treasured government scholarship. In Grade 9, I won an award as the school's 'best actor'. Seven years there culminated in my doing an academic programme heavily loaded with history in the Cambridge Higher School Certificate exams, administered, set and graded in the United Kingdom.

The three-point history component of my studies comprised British, European and American History. Ironically for the son of a passionate nationalist with great pride in Jamaican heritage, there was no such option as Jamaican History or Caribbean History.

Working near to the West India Reference Library in downtown Kingston shortly after my school days, I sought to fill this void by spending most of my lunch hours researching in that library. My attention was soon drawn to newspaper articles, mainly in *The Jamaica Gleaner* and *Galt's Daily News*, about a faith healer named Alexander Bedward whom I had known from oral history as a figure of ridicule. The Bedward I had heard of from early childhood was a late 19th-century/early 20th-century prophet who had attempted to fly to heaven and had broken a leg, an arm, or his neck in the attempt, the precise fate depending on the proximate source of the story. However, contemporary press reports revealed that, while Bedward announced that he would ascend into heaven, he postponed the scheduled flight five times, the last postponement being for seventeen years, of which he spent the following nine years until his death in a lunatic asylum.

There were, however, numerous news stories and editorials that revealed massive antagonism between Bedward and the establishment which he attributed to racial injustice and fear of his influence over the poor, black masses.

Among the documents in the library were the minutes of a conspiratorial meeting, hosted by the Governor at his official residence, King's House, and attended by such luminaries as the Attorney General, the police chief, and magistrate Sam Burke, who would try Bedward as he fell into the conspirators' well laid trap. Those minutes were consistent with Bedward's claim of race prejudice and fear of his influence, as were other documents found at the library.

In 1957, I paid my first visit to Bedward's headquarters in August Town to interview surviving Bedwardites. Thirty-six years had by then elapsed since his committal to the lunatic asylum after the security forces diverted his attempted march on Kingston 'for a manifestation' and delivered him into the hands of magistrate Sam Burke.

The entrance to the Bedward commune, Union Camp, was a narrow footpath with no sign of life – just an eerie silence – as I trod my lonely way toward the Camp. Suddenly, with still no visible sign of anyone, a stentorian voice announced: 'There is a stranger in our midst.' I felt unwelcome and emphatically vulnerable.

At the end of the path, I saw a handful of persons standing on a verandah, their body language suggesting that they were awaiting my arrival. One had an uncanny resemblance to the Bedward I had seen in photographs. My self-introduction was mannerly and respectful. The Bedward look-alike identified himself as the prophet's grandson, ironically surnamed Burke.

Early exchanges reflected a community of simple folk who considered themselves despised and persecuted by the wider society and had therefore withdrawn into their laager. Every outsider was suspect, including myself.

I adopted a new strategy, relating sympathetically what I had learnt about Bedward. As I reached back into history, before their lifetime, they seemed more receptive and welcoming, as if learning new, positive facts about their hero. I was encouraged to return whenever I chose. On my second visit, I was warmly welcomed, entertained and told the Bedward story from their perspective.

As a very active member of the continuously busy Caribbean Thespians Dramatic Society, which included such sublime talents as those of Charles Hyatt and Mona (Chin) Hammond, I made a successful debut as a playwright that year. I then added a Bedward drama to my to-do list.

In January 1960, the Jamaica Broadcasting Corporation (JBC) broadcast *The Shepherd*, my radio drama on Alexander Bedward. The producer was Robin Midgley, a young Englishman on loan from the BBC, who encouraged me to do a stage version, which premiered later that year at the Ward Theatre. Rewritten editions were presented later as *Bedward*.

Principal Cast

(in order of appearance)

BISHOP SHAKESPEARE WOODS

SISTER SARAH PLUNKETT

PASTOR ALEXANDER BEDWARD

MRS ALEXANDER BEDWARD

PASTOR DAWSON

PASTOR ROMAN HENRY

PASTOR STEELE

POLICE INSPECTOR WRIGHT

SGT MAJOR WILLIAMS

GOVERNOR OF JAMAICA

RESIDENT MAGISTRATE SAM BURKE

DR JOHN EDWARDS

ACT ONE
SCENE ONE	UNION CAMP
SCENE TWO	UNION CAMP
SCENE THREE	UNON CAMP
SCENE FOUR	HOPE RIVER
SCENE FIVE	HOPE RIVER
SCENE SIX	UNION CAMP
SCENE SEVEN	UNION CAMP
SCENE EIGHT	UNION CAMP
SCENE NINE	KING'S HOUSE
SCENE TEN	UNION CAMP

ACT TWO
SCENE ONE	UNION CAMP
SCENE TWO	UNION CAMP
SCENE THREE	MONA ROAD
SCENE FOUR	HALFWAY TREE COURT ROOM
SCENE FIVE	LOCK UP CELL
SCENE SIX	HALFWAY TREE COURT HOUSE
SCENE SEVEN	HALFWAY TREE COURT HOUSE

ACT ONE

SCENE I

(Union Camp, August Town. An ensemble opening with all cast members taking part singing and praising with 'Down in the Valley'. Enter SHAKESPEARE WOODS to a climax in the musical devotional celebrations.)

WOODS: My people, today I must leave you.

CONGREG: Oh, no!

WOODS: But only in the flesh. My spirit will always be here in August Town. As of now, Pastor Bedward will be your new Bishop.

CONGREG: Pastor Bedward?!

WOODS: You in this Church will face a savage struggle against the forces of evil outside. If you are to win the battle for good you must stand fully united behind Bishop Bedward.

SARAH: But why you going, Shakespeare?

ALL: Yes. Why?

WOODS: At the age of 91 and after three years as your Bishop it's time for me to make way for a younger man.

SARAH: So where you going?

ALL: Yes. Where?

WOODS: Never mind me. Just be obedient to Bishop Bedward. Blessed are those who die in the Lord though not baptised. They attain unto the first heaven through the blood. More blessed are those who die in the Lord and were baptised. They attain unto the second heaven through his love. More blessed are those who die in the Lord and were baptised and in obedience to Bishop Bedward, whom God has sent, or to the Holy Spirit in their hearts, devote themselves to fasting. They attain

143

unto the third heaven through obedience… My people, I
who have foretold the death of men and the destruction
of villages now prophesy that this man, Alexander
Bedward, will be the leader of a great religious
movement centred here in August Town; that fruits will
so abound in August Town that from various parts of the
world people will come to gather them.

*SHAKESPEARE WOODS goes, assisted by BEDWARD. The
CONGREGATION wave goodbye, singing 'I Can Hear the Saviour
Calling'. The CONGREGATION hum as the two bishops converse.*

BEDWARD: You see why I expressed doubts about succeeding
you, Bishop? Did you observe the reaction of the
congregation? They were clearly disappointed, not only
with your retirement, but even more so with the choice
of your successor.

WOODS: Give them a little time. They'll be fully supportive.

BEDWARD: But Bishop, how can I take your place? My life
has been blighted by sin and vice. Your whole life has
been dedicated to God's work. You have lived as a
hermit, denying yourself all the comforts and pleasures
of the world. You have been a great prophet. When you
said there would be a flood the heavens broke. When
you warned that people would die they went swiftly to
their graves. You founded this Church out of nothing,
Shakespeare Woods. You enlisted a membership and
wrote the services. I have neither the education nor the
moral strength to carry on such work.

WOODS: You are a man of great gifts, Alexander Bedward. If
you use them in service of your people you will not only
save your own soul but be the means of saving others.
The choice is yours. You can have a bleak future or you
can shine like the brightest star in the galaxy of heaven.

BEDWARD: How can I do that?

WOODS: Bring order to a disordered life. Rid your loins of
lust. Insulate your palms against any tendency to itch.
Give up all worldly vice and all excess. Forsake not

innocent passion, but never let anger overcome you or take control of your actions. Be the calm in the eye of the storm. Show courage and humility. Distribute praise liberally and take all blame unto yourself. Lead through the personal example of rigid discipline. Work like a colony of bees to achieve what you believe in. Broaden your mind and sharpen your wit through study. Be gentle and kind to others. Be honest and sincere in all your dealings. Try this simple test upon yourself. Look every man squarely in the eye and when you can do so without flinching you will be a true leader of men. Then you will be able to stare into the sun itself. Above all else, remember that the Lord Jesus Christ did not walk with princes. He lived and died for the poor of the world. And He still lives. For he who reigns by love is sustained by love... *(Pause.)* ...Agreed?

BEDWARD: Yes, Bishop.

WOODS: Then you will be a great Bishop of the Jamaica Native Baptist Free Church.

BEDWARD: But, Bishop, will I get the support of the other elders? Take Pastor Dawson for instance. He has led a very devout, humble and upright life. He has been a senior elder and pastor of the Church for a long time. My life can't compare with his. Why shouldn't he be the Bishop?

WOODS: Some men are naturally excellent lieutenants but will never be good commanders. I informed Pastor Dawson of my choice and he fully understands and has pledged his support. As Moses and Aaron stood before the congregation of Israel, so will you and Pastor Dawson stand here as one before the people. You should not have any problems within the Church. Your main opposition will be from without. Keep a close watch on the gateway to your temple.

SHAKESPEARE WOODS disappears. The CONGREGATION becomes still. Out of the darkness comes SARAH to take her vow.

BEDWARD: Sister Sarah Plunkett, are you at peace?

SARAH: Yes, Shepherd.

BEDWARD: Take this candle, kneel and repeat the vow after me.

She takes candle; kneels.

BEDWARD: Lord, have mercy on me.

SARAH: Lord, have mercy on me.

BEDWARD: Christ, have mercy on me.

SARAH: Christ, have mercy on me.

BEDWARD: Oh, God, be pleased to show me my sin and my condemnation.

SARAH: Oh, God, be pleased to show me my sin and my condemnation.

BEDWARD: Help me to flee from my sin and do it no more.

SARAH: Help me to flee from my sin and do it no more.

BEDWARD: For Jesus Christ's sake.

SARAH: For Jesus Christ's sake.

BEDWARD/SARAH: Amen.

The CONGREGATION sing. As SARAH leaves altar, she crosses with MRS BEDWARD.

SCENE II

Union Camp at night. Sound of crickets and tree frogs. A lonely and pensive BEDWARD paces the yard, eventually sits on platform. MRS BEDWARD emerges from house, walks down to BEDWARD.

MRS BED: What happen, Alexander? You not coming to bed tonight?

BEDWARD: Please, I want to be alone.

MRS BED: *(Putting arm round him.)* Why? What's wrong?

BEDWARD: Don't touch me.

MRS BED: You? Don't want me to touch you? What's the matter?

BEDWARD: I been called by God to do a special job.

MRS BED: So...?

BEDWARD: I have to come well prepared for my mission. I have to purify myself; to renounce all flesh.

MRS BED: Alexander, I am your wife.

BEDWARD: That makes no difference. Flesh is flesh.

MRS BED: Flesh is flesh, eh? That's why you were never very choosey about which, or whose.

BEDWARD: That is in the past. But now, all flesh is out of bounds, married or single. That means that from now on you and I will not sleep in the same bed.

MRS BED: So who will sleep in the same bed as you? Sister Sarah Plunkett?

BEDWARD: Hold your tongue, Woman.

MRS BED: Which of the sisters? Eh? Which of them?

BEDWARD: Don't you understand what I'm saying?

MRS BED: No, I don't. You think I'm a fool, Alexander. You think I don't know about you and some of the women in the church.

BEDWARD: You're talking history. I'm dealing with the present. And now, because I have been specially chosen by God to do his most important work, because I must lead by example, I must give up flesh.

MRS BED: Give up flesh, I agree, but not your wife. I'm sure that's not God's wish.

BEDWARD: You wouldn't understand God's wish. You are of the world.

MRS BED: You don't dare talk to me like that. You are forgetting a few facts about your life.

BEDWARD: You are still living in the past. What has gone before cannot be cancelled, but it is ended. Now I stand at a milestone in my life. The journey ahead is rough. It is a journey I am undertaking for God, and I cannot carry the burden of flesh with me. So for the future no flesh; which means, no you, Mrs Bedward.

SCENE III

MRS BED: Good morning, Pastor Dawson.

DAWSON: Good morning, Mrs Bedward.

MRS BED: So, how do you feel about your new Bishop, Pastor Dawson?

DAWSON: I beg your pardon, Mrs Bedward...!

MRS BED: Come, come, Pastor Dawson. Remember, nobody knows Alexander Bedward better than I...and I can't see him as Bishop.

DAWSON: God moves in a mysterious way.

MRS BED: Very mysterious, it seems.

DAWSON: You shouldn't be talking like this, Mrs Bedward.

MRS BED: Fair is fair, Pastor Dawson. There is none fitter than you to be the new Bishop of this Church.

DAWSON: But, Mrs Bedward!

MRS BED: Certainly not Alexander Bedward.

DAWSON: Please, say no more.

MRS BED: Look at the life he has led and compare the personal sacrifices you have made throughout your life in the name of God.

DAWSON: And I have one more sacrifice to make – one more act of self-denial to perform in the name of God. I must support Bishop Bedward as Shakespeare Woods commanded.

MRS BED: Bishop Bedward, eh? It doesn't even sound right.

DAWSON: Why are you doing this to your husband, Mrs Bedward? You should be fighting for him; not against.

MRS BED: I am just talking the truth as I see it. There is too much sin in the man.

DAWSON: But his sin was purged out of him with his visions in Colon when he was scourged and told to return to Jamaica.

MRS BED: Visions in Colon! You really believe that? Pastor Dawson, you're a true Christian and a righteous man. It's a pity for the Church that you are so innocent.

PASTORS and ELDERS take up positions at altar. BEDWARD and HENRY stop by DAWSON and MRS BEDWARD.

DAWSON: Good morning, Bishop Bedward.

BEDWARD does not answer. He stares at DAWSON silently for a long time.

DAWSON: Good morning, Pastor Henry. *(HENRY does not answer.)*

BEDWARD: Pastor Dawson, we are about to start the meeting of pastors and elders, if you care to join us.

DAWSON: *(Obviously taken aback by apparent hostility.)* Of course.

BEDWARD and HENRY walk past DAWSON and MRS BEDWARD.

MRS BED: Pastor Dawson, it looks like somebody is afraid of you. Maybe you are regarded as a threat because you have better qualifications.

DAWSON: Your husband and I are not rivals, Mrs Bedward. We are a team.

MRS BED: But watch that Pastor Henry. He plays on other men's vanity. That type is dangerous for Alexander Bedward.

DAWSON: I'm sorry Mrs Bedward. I have to join the other pastors and elders, so will you please excuse me now.

MRS BED: Of course, Pastor.

PASTOR DAWSON goes to join PASTORS and ELDERS. MRS BEDWARD looks at him with pity.

BEDWARD: My dear Pastors, you heard our beloved founder speak of a great religious movement centred in August Town.

HENRY: Yes, Shepherd.

BEDWARD: I have had a vision.

DAWSON: *(Expectantly.)* Yes, Shepherd.

BEDWARD: In this vision, I saw Shakespeare Woods' prophecy come true. I saw the people come here in their hundreds and thousands to be fed and clothed and to worship God.

DAWSON: Worshipping is one thing, Shepherd…but feeding and clothing…?

BEDWARD: Ah, Pastor Dawson, we have a great job to do here. We must start with what we have – the land in Union Camp. And we must put our backs behind the hoe to produce from the soil so that we can feed the poor.

DAWSON: But, Shepherd, our business is the word of God. Time spent in agriculture is time lost to God's teachings.

BEDWARD: Those who don't wish to work the soil are free not to work it, Pastor Dawson. But I shall lead whoever will join me…and every morning before the sun is up we shall pray and then we shall till the soil. Who is with me?

HENRY: I, Shepherd.

BEDWARD: Pastor Steele?

STEELE: Oh yes, Shepherd.

BEDWARD: Pastor Dawson…?

DAWSON: Oh, I have no objection to working the soil, Shepherd; don't get me wrong. I just want to be assured that we never lose sight of our real mission, which is the word of God.

BEDWARD: The work of God is more important than the word of God, Pastor Dawson.

DAWSON: Shepherd.

BEDWARD: *(Staring him down.)* Yes, Pastor Dawson.

DAWSON: *(Flinching.)* Oh, nothing.

BEDWARD: My dear Pastors, you know that my past life has been by no means perfect.

HENRY: No man is perfect, Shepherd.

BEDWARD: But from today I intend to follow closely in the footsteps of our teacher Shakespeare Woods and of the Lord Jesus Christ. I renounce all things of the flesh, all vice and all excess. We are going to have a great battle in this Church against the forces of evil, and I must prepare myself for the battle.

DAWSON: What battle is this you speak of, Shepherd?

BEDWARD: The battle against those who are against the poor that we must stand for.

DAWSON: But why do we have to stand only for the poor, Shepherd?

BEDWARD: The others can stand for themselves.

DAWSON: But that is not so. Remember, our Lord Jesus Christ said it is easier for a camel to pass through the eye of a needle than for a rich man to enter into Kingdom of God.

BEDWARD: The rich have their own churches, Pastor Dawson. The Pope of Rome and the Archbishop of Canterbury take good care of them.

DAWSON: That's not entirely true, Shepherd. There are many rich people who are lost. We can win them for God. And we need them as much as we need the poor. After all, the Church needs money to survive.

BEDWARD: The Lord will provide.

DAWSON: God helps those who help themselves, Shepherd.

BEDWARD: It seems, Pastor Dawson, that for once Shakespeare Woods was wrong when he said that I would have the full support of the leaders of the Church.

DAWSON: You're not being fair to me, Shepherd.

BEDWARD: Who is not with me is against me, Dawson.

DAWSON: Shepherd.

BEDWARD: And those who can't follow loyally and obediently can worship elsewhere.

DAWSON: It is not the worship I worry about, Shepherd. It's the other things.

BEDWARD: In this Church, the needs of the body and the spirit are one. In the white man's church they can separate these things. They come to service well fed. In the Jamaica Native Baptist Free Church we have to be concerned about the condition of the poor. You agree, Pastor Henry?

HENRY: Oh yes, Shepherd.

BEDWARD: You see, Dawson? There is a loyal and obedient servant of God.

DAWSON shrugs sadly. BEDWARD stares him in the eye. DAWSON flinches.

SCENE IV

Hope River. BEDWARD stands alone, black rod in hand, staring into the sun for a considerable time. He is joined by HENRY. HENRY is clearly taken aback by BEDWARD's stare into the sun

HENRY: Why are you staring into the sun like that, Shepherd?

BEDWARD: *(Still staring.)* I want to see which of us will bow, Pastor Henry. Shakespeare Woods told me if I could look every man squarely in the eye without flinching I could stare into the sun itself.

HENRY: But it can't be good for your eyes, Shepherd.

BEDWARD: Don't worry about my eyes, Pastor Henry. Worry about the sun.

HENRY: If you can stare at the sun like that, Shepherd, you can do just about anything.

BEDWARD: You're so right, Pastor Henry. And in just a little while you'll see that manifested.

The CONGREGATION are heard, off, approaching singing.

BEDWARD: And the Lord leads me to a certain spot in the Hope River, and says unto me: 'Once I made water wine. Behold, now I make water medicine. And you, Alexander Bedward, I have ordained my dispenser, watchman, shepherd and trumpeter.'

ALL: Amen.

BEDWARD: Who is here that cannot see? Who is dumb or lame or halt? Who is sick in body or mind? Come forward. Come with Pastor Henry.

A BLIND WOMAN is guided to HENRY. A CRIPPLE is pushed forward in his wheelchair. A DEAF WOMAN is signalled to go; and a DUMB MAN goes forward making signs that he cannot speak. The others talk to HENRY. There is a murmur among the CONGREGATION.

HENRY: One cannot see, one cannot hear, one cannot speak, and one cannot walk.

BEDWARD turns towards the sun, his arms held horizontal, the black rod in his right hand.

SARAH: The Shepherd looking straight into the sun.

WOMAN: Him not batting a eyelid.

SARAH: The Shepherd is sent by God to save us.

BEDWARD turns around to face the CONGREGATION, looks at the AFFLICTED.

BEDWARD: In the name of the Father, of the Son and of the Holy Ghost, I command the Devil to leave your body... Be thou made whole by the healing balm of this blessed stream.

BEDWARD dips the heads of the DEAF and the MUTE.

MUTE: I can talk. Praise the Lord, I can talk

DEAF: I can hear. I hear you, Brother. You say, 'I can talk.'

ALL: *(Led by SARAH.)* Praise the Lord! Glory! Halleluyah!

HENRY: *(Raising song.)* Let the power fall on me, Shepherd.

CONGREGATION: *(Joining singing.)*

> Let the power fall on me.
>
> Let the power fall on me, Shepherd.
>
> Let the power fall on me.
>
> You give me justice, peace and love, Shepherd.
>
> You give me justice, peace and love.
>
> Now let the power fall on me, Shepherd.
>
> Let the power fall on me.

BEDWARD: In the name of the Father, of the Son and of the Holy Ghost, I command the Devil to leave your body… Be thou made whole by the healing balm of this blessed stream.

BEDWARD dips the heads of the CRIPPLE and the BLIND. The BLIND throws away her stick.

BLIND: *(Running about.)* I can see! I can see!

CRIPPLE leaps to his feet and hoists his wheelchair above his head, dancing around.

BEDWARD: 'Go and tell every man what things ye have seen and heard; how the blind see, the lame walk, the sick are healed, the deaf hear and to the poor the gospel is preached…and blessed is he whosoever shall not be offended in me.'

CONGREG: *(Singing, led by SARAH.)*

> Let the power fall on me, Shepherd
>
> Oh, let the power fall on me.
>
> Let the power you bring from up above,
>
> Let the power fall on me.
>
> You give me justice, peace and love, Shepherd.
>
> You give me justice, peace and love.
>
> Now let the power you bring from up above,
>
> Let the power fall on me.

SCENE V

Hope River. The same as previous scene. The CONGREGATION are singing 'Let The Power Fall, etc.' The GOVERNMENT CHEMIST enters, accompanied by POLICE INSPECTOR WRIGHT and SGT MAJOR WILLIAMS. The singing fades into silence.

BEDWARD: Go on singing, Children. What's happened to your voices?

Singing starts again, led by SARAH, very uncertainly now.

BEDWARD: Come on... Sing! *(He leads the song.)*

INSPECTOR: Excuse me a moment, please... I take it you are Mr Bedward.

BEDWARD: That's right.

INSPECTOR: We've heard certain things about your stream, Mr Bedward, and thought it might be a good idea to bring the Government Chemist to take samples of your water *(Sarcastically.)* if you don't mind, Mr Bedward.

BEDWARD: Not at all... There is enough left for him to take a bottle or two.

By now there is a considerable group of JOURNALISTS, PHOTOGRAPHERS, DOCTORS and CLERICS, all distinguished by the trappings of their various occupations.

INSPECTOR: Thank you, Bishop.

BEDWARD: It takes a lot of people to carry two bottles of water, eh, Inspector?

(CONGREGATION laughs.)...Or perhaps they are just jealous of the power of Alexander Bedward to take plain water from the stream and heal all manner of illness... Doctors and priests, aren't they, Inspector?

Racketeers who are jealous of my power because it denies them the chance to rob our poor black brothers. Newspaper reporters, prostitutes who will make sensation of anything to satisfy their lust for mammon...

(Pause... There is pure silence.) ...Ah, my children! There is a black wall and a white wall, and the white wall has been closing round the black wall. But now the black wall is growing, and it shall crush the white wall *(Tremendous crowd reaction.)* I know the white men of this country, the Pharisees and Sadducees, won't like me because I teach the word to the poor and because I expose their iniquity; for the Lord said, 'We have prophesied in thy name, and in thy name have cast out devils and in thy name done many wonderful works; and then will I profess unto them. I never knew you. Depart from me, ye that work iniquity.'

Great emotional reaction from CONGREGATION.

GOVERNMENT CHEMIST, INSPECTOR, DOCTORS, REPORTERS go.

'Unless ye be converted and become as little children...'

ALL: Ye shall not enter into the Kingdom of God.

BEDWARD: Blessed are ye when men shall hate you and when they shall separate you from their company and cast out your name as evil, for the Son of Man's sake. Rejoice ye in that day, and leap for joy. For, behold, your reward is great in heaven. For in like manner...

ALL: Did their fathers unto the prophets.

BEDWARD: Your reward is great in heaven. But we may not have to wait for death to get to heaven, for if a man have enough faith he will be able to fly like the birds. Fly away over the heads of our enemies. They better stop troubling me or I will fly.

SARAH: Fly! Fly! Fly!

CONGREG: Fly! Fly! Fly!

HENRY: *(Starts singing.)* 'Don't You Trouble Shepherd'.

The CONGREGATION take up the song. They exit singing. Singing fades into distance.

BEDWARD remains in his place. He is joined by MRS BEDWARD.

MRS BED: Alexander, you really must not make enemies of all those powerful people.

BEDWARD: Watch your tongue, Woman. I make enemies with no one. I am merely carrying out the Lord's work.

MRS BED: But you called them racketeers, prostitutes, robbers...

BEDWARD: They are. Didn't you see who they were?

MRS BED: But if you attack them like that they'll make life impossible for you.

BEDWARD: What is this to do with you, Woman?

MRS BED: I'm still your wife.

BEDWARD: You are flesh, that's what you are; a carnal beast, and I will have nothing more to do with flesh.

MRS BED: I just thought I'd warn you. And, by the way, those pastors and elders you have around you... Most of them are no good...just riff-raff. The only exception is Pastor Dawson.

BEDWARD: Begone!

MRS BED: All right, Alexander, but remember. If you continue to rely on those elders you and your Church will come to grief.

BEDWARD: Away, vile woman. Jezebel!

BEDWARD lifts his rod. MRS BEDWARD goes quietly. HENRY passes her. They exchange mean looks. HENRY approaches BEDWARD.

HENRY: What happen to you, Shepherd? You not leaving the stream today?

BEDWARD: Pastor Henry... I'm so glad to see you. You see how we have to fight against the forces of darkness, Henry?

HENRY: Ah, Shepherd.

BEDWARD: You hear the latest? They refused me a licence to marry the brothers and sisters in my own Church. So the

brothers and sisters must go into pagan churches to be
married by the priests of the Pope and the Archbishop
of Canterbury. Hell will be their portion. I, Alexander
Bedward, going to see that they burn in the fires of hell.

HENRY: Yeah, Shepherd. Burn. Burn.

SCENE VI

*Union Camp. A well guarded gate now downstage left. All BROTHERS
and SISTERS are seated on the ground. There are baskets of food placed
among the flock. Outside the gate are the INSPECTOR, the SGT MAJOR
and NEWSPAPER REPORTER.*

BEDWARD: A hungry saint make a wicked sinner! Pastor
Henry, are all at peace?

HENRY: Yes, Shepherd.

BEDWARD: Feed my people.

HENRY: In the name of the Father, of the Son and of the Holy
Ghost, Amen.

The food is distributed.

SARAH: The Shepherd heal the sick and feed the multitude.
The Shepherd is sent by God to save us. God save the
Shepherd. Long live the Shepherd!

BEDWARD: God will provide, Brothers and Sisters. With God's
good guidance we take from those who can give and give
to those who need.

REPORTER: Good morning, Brother.

PORTER: *(At gate.)* Morning.

REPORTER: I'd like to see Mr Bedward, please.

PORTER: Who you?

REPORTER: My name is Bennett. I'm a *Gleaner* reporter.

PORTER: The Shepherd doan' waan' si no damn *Gleaner*
reporter.

REPORTER: Don't you think that's a decision he should take
himself?

PORTER: Him tek it aready. Him doan' waan' si no damn
   Gleaner reporter.

REPORTER: May I see Mr Dawson?

PORTER: *(Pointing.)* Si him there.

REPORTER: If you don't mind, I'd like to have a word with
   him.

PORTER: Sorry.

REPORTER: *(Calling.)* Mr Dawson…Mr Dawson.

DAWSON: Somebody call me?

REPORTER: Over here, Mr Dawson.

DAWSON: *(Going to REPORTER.)* Yes…? What can I do for you?

REPORTER: I am Bennett, a reporter from the *Daily Gleaner*. I
   am very impressed with Mr Bedward's work and would
   like to interview him.

DAWSON: The *Daily Gleaner* is not very popular here, Mr
   Bennett. They have written some harsh things about the
   Shepherd and his Church.

REPORTER: I know, Sir, but I'm on your side. I can do
   something to correct the bad impressions that have been
   made by some earlier reports.

DAWSON: *(To PORTER.)* Let him in.

   *PORTER opens gate for Reporter, who enters. DAWSON takes him
   to BEDWARD.*

DAWSON: Shepherd, this is Mr Bennett, a reporter from the
   Gleaner.

BEDWARD: *Gleaner* reporter? And you bring him to me?
   Whose side are you on, Dawson?

DAWSON: It's not a matter of sides, Shepherd.

BEDWARD: Not a matter of sides? Bishop Gordon,
   representative of the Pope in Jamaica, issued a
   proclamation forbidding all Roman Catholics from
   coming to my healing stream and from encouraging
   others to come to the stream. Today the Anglican

Bishop, Enos Nuttall, is leading a march in Kingston against Bedwardism. And why all the opposition? Because Bishop Gordon and Bishop Nuttall have lost hold of their members. They cannot enter their souls. They can only understand the few white people whose souls they wish to save. They are apart from the many poor black people of Jamaica who are my people. They have not heeded the word of Joel, Chapter Two, verse twenty-nine: 'And also upon the servants and upon the handmaids in those days will I pour out my spirit'... Yes, Brethren. You see those clouds up there? Can you see the angels in the clouds?... You don't see them? Well, I can see angels in the clouds and they are telling me what I am telling you now. The ministers are thieves and liars and worship the anti-Christ. I am the true servant of the true Christ. Here are constables, detectives and inspectors. I defy them to arrest me. They may kill the body but they can't kill the soul. Let them come here and arrest me. They can't do it. I laugh at them and defy them.

SGT MAJOR is about to move.

INSPECTOR: No, Sergeant Major. Leave him alone.

SGT MAJOR: But, Inspector, the man has committed sedition.

INSPECTOR: Let's not play into his hands. Let him play into ours.

BEDWARD: The Government passes laws that oppress black people. They take their money out of their pocket and they rob them of their bread. The Government are thieves and liars and the Governor is a scoundrel and a robber.

SGT MAJOR: This is worse than sedition. This is treason. We have enough evidence against this man to have him hanged.

INSPECTOR: We must choose the right moment. Be patient, Sergeant Major.

BEDWARD: They have a force of military and constabulary
men, but what can they do to me? Nothing. For I have
the love of my people and therefore no force on earth
can stop Alexander Bedward.

*BEDWARD leads FOLLOWERS in singing 'Don't You Trouble
Shepherd'.*

SCENE VII

*Union Camp. BEDWARD, with newspaper in hand, addresses the
CONGREGATION.*

BEDWARD: You see how the Jamaica Native Baptist Free
Church has grown in the face of the most violent
opposition. We have fed the hungry and given succour
to the sick in body and mind. Here in Union Camp are
poor, deprived black people who had no purpose in life.

SARAH: *(Shouting.)* True, Shepherd.

BEDWARD: They just looked on as spectators at the world
happening around them. But now, in the Jamaica Native
Baptist Free Church, they are given something to live for.
Because we have given hope to poor black people, and
because we enjoy their loyalty and love, the authorities
will not cease harassing us. Look at the article by the
Gleaner reporter, Pastor Dawson's friend.

DAWSON: He's not my friend, Shepherd.

BEDWARD: *(Dismissing DAWSON.)* Peter denied the Lord Jesus
Christ himself, and Judas betrayed Him. Hear the report
from Pastor Dawson's friend: *(Reading.)*

'The scenes back of Long Mountain, a few miles from
where Columbus first planted civilisation in the New
World, continue, and they are scenes rivalling those of
darkest superstition in any part of the Old World.' And
he writes also about 'dirty filthy water and disgusting
scenes'; that our hymns are an excuse for dancing that
features 'pornographic undulations of the pelvic region
of the body'. And he claims that we indulge in wild
orgies here in Union Camp. *(Considerable agitation among*

161

the CONGREGATION.) ...What do you say we should do unto our enemies outside the gate?

HENRY: Call for a plague.

ALL: A plague upon them.

HENRY: *(Looking meanly at DAWSON.)* What about traitors within the gates, Shepherd?

BEDWARD: I shall deal personally with them, Pastor Henry.

HENRY: *(Singing.)* Press along, Shepherd, press along, in God's own way.

ALL: *(Singing.)* Press along, Shepherd, press along in God's own way.

Persecution you must bear,

Trial and crosses in your way.

Oh, the hotter the battle,

the sweeter the victory.

BEDWARD: Remember, if a man have enough faith he can do any thing. He can even fly like the birds.

SARAH: Fly! Fly!

ALL: *(Chanting.)* Fly! Fly! Fly!

BEDWARD: Now let me tell you about a great task that God has set us. Behold, the Lord has commanded me to build Him a magnificent temple, the finest structure in the western hemisphere, and there we shall worship Him. The church will be ninety-one feet long, sixty-one feet wide and twenty-four feet high. It will be a solid building of cut stones built with two floors and with galleries on three sides. The pulpit will be nearly fifteen feet high. And we, brothers and sisters of the church, shall ourselves erect this magnificent structure. All of us.

MAN: But I don't know nothing 'bout building, Shepherd.

BEDWARD: Faith, Brother. All you need is faith. The Lord will provide.

SARAH: *(Starts song.)* Press along, Shepherd, press along, in God's own way.

ALL: *(Singing.)* Press along, Shepherd, press along in God's own way.

Persecution you must bear.

Trial and crosses in your way.

Oh, the hotter the battle,

the sweeter the victory.

CONGREGATION have formed themselves into a chain gang, passing stones. One MAN mixes mortar, MASONS erect wall of Church.

ALL: *(Singing.)* Press along, Shepherd, press along. In God's own way. Press along Shepherd, press along in God's own way. Persecution you must bear, Trial and crosses in your way. Oh, the hotter the battle, the sweeter the victory.

CONGREGATION hum.

BEDWARD: Yes my Children, work like you have never worked before. Let this temple be a monument to our defiance of the white sepulchre. Let it be a witness to what our poor black brothers and sisters can achieve even in the face of the most violent oppression.

ALL: *(Singing.)* Press along, Shepherd, press along, in God's own way. Press along Shepherd, press along in God's own way. Persecution you must bear, Trial and crosses in your way. Oh, the hotter the battle, the sweeter the victory.

DAWSON walks away. MRS BEDWARD joins him.

MRS BED: You see how the game is being played, Pastor Dawson? Now you've been pushed into Number Three position…and Mr Roman Henry sits on the right hand of the Shepherd.

DAWSON: I don't care about those things, Mrs Bedward.

MRS BED: *(With pity.)* Such a Christian, Pastor Dawson.

HENRY walks down within earshot of DAWSON and MRS BEDWARD.

MRS BED: Pastor Henry.

HENRY: Yes, Mrs Bedward.

MRS BED: How are the finances of the Church?

HENRY: I'm afraid I don't understand the question.

MRS BED: *(Sampling his collar.)* Nice clothes you're wearing… Look expensive.

HENRY: So this is what you spend your time doing, Pastor Dawson. Indulging in idle gossip.

DAWSON: I haven't said a word, Pastor Henry.

HENRY: I consider it my duty to tell the Shepherd.

DAWSON: But I never…

HENRY: To let him know what his trusted Pastor is up to. Good day to you, Pastor Dawson… *(No reply.)*…and good day to you, Mrs Bedward.

SCENE VIII

Union Camp. Late night. BEDWARD, in pyjamas, paces yard, walks down to gate.

BEDWARD: *(To PORTER.)* Brother, you seen any sign of Mrs Bedward?

PORTER: She went out about an hour ago, Shepherd.

BEDWARD: And Pastor Dawson?

PORTER: He went about twenty minutes later.

BEDWARD: Why didn't you stop them?

PORTER: I don't have any authority to stop them, Shepherd.

BEDWARD: I guess you're right…I don't like it at all. There's a nasty feeling in the air. Guard the gate well, Brother. And don't allow anyone in or out.

PORTER: Yes, Shepherd.

BEDWARD goes behind house. INSPECTOR, SGT MAJOR and POLICEMEN approach PORTER.

PORTER: No one is allowed in.

INSPECTOR: *(Pushing his stick across PORTER's mouth.)* Not a squeak out of you. Corporal Sutton, stay close to him.

CORPORAL: Yes, Sir.

INSPECTOR and OTHER POLICEMEN go towards house. Presently BEDWARD emerges.

BEDWARD: Who is it?

INSPECTOR: Good evening Mr Bedward.

BEDWARD: Good night, Inspector.

INSPECTOR: I have a warrant for your arrest.

BEDWARD: But why so many men? If you had sent a child I would have come. And why the arms, Inspector?

INSPECTOR: You said we dare not arrest you. We had to ensure you wouldn't be tempted to prove the point.

BEDWARD: I see... May I ask what the charge is, Inspector?

INSPECTOR: Making seditious utterances... Read this.

INSPECTOR takes document from SGT MAJOR, holds it, with light, for BEDWARD to read.

BEDWARD: But that's a lie! I never said any of these things. You've used my own words and twisted them.

INSPECTOR: Save your story for the Judge. Come.

POLICEMEN are carrying BEDWARD off.

BEDWARD: Can't I even change my clothes?

INSPECTOR: Not necessary. We provide clothing, free of charge.

SARAH, ROMAN HENRY and OTHERS sing 'Don't You Trouble Shepherd'.

SCENE IX

King's House. Half Way Tree Resident Magistrate Sam Burke is meeting with Governor Probyn, with the Governor's Secretary in attendance.

GOVERNOR: But how not guilty, Mr Burke? The man's clearly a menace to law and order.

BURKE: He had a clever lawyer, Mr Philip Stern.

GOVERNOR: Oh, Stern!

BURKE: Who shot holes in the Crown's case.

GOVERNOR: But what's to be done about the man Bedward?

BURKE: First, Your Excellency, as the Attorney General has advised, we should guard against giving any impression that Bedward is the victim of state persecution. That's the impression that Stern is cunningly trying to create, that these people's human rights are being violated by the state. And regrettably he seems to have convinced a considerable number of well-meaning but naïve people that it is so. I would add, Sir, that when next a charge is laid against Bedward the evidence should be irrefutable. And with regard to that point it were best that any Crown evidence should be supported by a member of his Church, preferably by one of his elders.

GOVERNOR: Thank you, Mr Burke. *(To his secretary.)* Ask the guard to show in Mr Dawson. I'm not entirely comfortable, Mr Burke, with the advice of the Inspector General of Police that we shouldn't take action against Bedward and his followers as long as they remain behind the gates of Union Camp but that we should deal with them only if and when they venture outside. That sounds too much like a concession that Bedward is above the law and that August Town, or Union Camp, is a state within a state, and out of bounds to the Police.

BURKE: With all due respect, Sir, I don't think that's what the Police chief is suggesting. His concern is about Stern's cunning propaganda.

GOVERNOR: I've got the point.

SECRETARY: Your Excellency, this is Pastor Dawson.

DAWSON enters diffidently.

GOVERNOR: Oh, Pastor Dawson. Welcome. This is the Resident Magistrate for St Andrew, Mr Samuel Burke

(Greetings exchanged.) and you've met my Secretary. Shall I pour you a cup of tea, Pastor Dawson?

DAWSON: No, thank you, Sir.

GOVERNOR: Oh, come on, Mr Dawson. Have a cup of tea.

DAWSON: Yes, thank you, Sir.

GOVERNOR pours tea.

GOVERNOR: Yes, Pastor Dawson. We live in troubled times, don't we?

DAWSON: Yes, Sir.

GOVERNOR: Where is it all going to end, I ask myself.

DAWSON: That's a very good question, Your Excellency.

GOVERNOR: You tell me, Pastor Dawson. You know the scene well. I gather you have been with the Church since its inception.

DAWSON: Yes, Sir.

BURKE: What about the prospects of an outbreak of violence in August Town, Pastor Dawson?

DAWSON: If I sin God forgive me, but what I shall say now I say because I see a great danger to peace in the island and to the way of life we all hold dear. What is happening at August Town, Your Excellency, is that respect for authority is breaking down, hatred is being preached, and the seeds of division sown.

GOVERNOR: Well said, Pastor Dawson.

BURKE: It has been reported, Pastor Dawson, that there has also been an erosion of moral standards.

GOVERNOR: Yes, there's much talk of orgies.

DAWSON: I haven't experienced any of that, Sir.

BURKE: But if there were orgies you wouldn't have to be personally involved, would you, Pastor Dawson?

DAWSON: No, Sir.

BURKE: I have it on good authority that the dance movements that accompany their songs are very erotic. Not what you would expect from people professing to be Christians. And incidents have been reported of young unmarried girls having babies.

DAWSON: There have been one or two such cases, Sir.

GOVERNOR: Whose babies? The Shepherd and his elders?

DAWSON: I don't think so, Your Excellency. Bishop Bedward is very strict on moral questions.

BURKE: Come, come, Pastor Dawson, it's an open secret that Bedward can have any woman he wants in Union Camp; that if he sees a married woman he fancies, her husband has to surrender her to Bedward. And the same applies to their young daughters. He has an awesome reputation for lascivious living. His exploits are a legend in August Town, Papine, Liguanea and Mona.

BURKE: In fairness to Bishop Bedward, Gentlemen, his personal life has changed a great deal since those days. Anything you've heard otherwise are just malicious lies. He has tried to set a good example and he demands high standards of morality, discipline and hard work from those in the Church.

GOVERNOR: How many wives does he have?

DAWSON: Only one, Sir. And they're estranged.

GOVERNOR: Estranged why?

DAWSON: I haven't tried to find out. With all due respect, Sir, I regard that as their private business.

GOVERNOR: So if he's as morally upright as you claim, Pastor Dawson, why are you uncomfortable in the Church? What's the problem?

DAWSON: He won't stick to religion. He keeps dragging what I would call 'politics' into the mission of the Church.

BURKE: Disgraceful.

GOVERNOR: We don't meddle in his spiritual affairs, so why does he want to dabble in what is clearly our business?

BURKE: Ambition.

GOVERNOR: How many followers does he have, Pastor Dawson?

DAWSON: There are five or six thousand who worship at August Town, Your Excellency.

GOVERNOR: *(Alarmed.)* Five or six thousand!

DAWSON: That's not all, Sir. There are many more in other parts of Jamaica, in Costa Rica, Cuba and the United States of America.

GOVERNOR: But how could there be this following outside Jamaica, even in a civilised country like the United States?

DAWSON: Mainly through the healing power of Bishop Bedward, Your Excellency. Articles have been written in newspapers and magazines abroad and many foreigners have come to the stream and have been healed.

GOVERNOR: I never knew that. Did you know of these things, Mr Burke?

BURKE: Of the healing itself, yes, Sir. But as for the numbers, with all respect to Pastor Dawson, I have my doubts. In an island like Jamaica, so prone to gossip and rumour, one has to sift carefully what one believes. In any case, we mustn't overestimate Bedward's importance. The people he appeals to abroad are the same class of people he appeals to in Jamaica – the poor, backward negro people.

GOVERNOR: How many followers does he have altogether, Pastor Dawson?

DAWSON: More than thirty thousand, Sir.

GOVERNOR: More than thirty thousand?! The man is dangerous. It's time to end this madness.

BURKE: With deference, Your Excellency, I believe if we give Bedward enough rope…

GOVERNOR: He might hang all of us. He has got to be stopped now.

BURKE: Your Excellency, we must not make a martyr of this man.

GOVERNOR: So what do you advise, Mr Burke?

BURKE: Bedward is a gambler, Sir. As he wins one game he raises the stake for the next. One of these days he will raise the stakes too high and then his whole kingdom will come crashing at his feet.

GOVERNOR: And who will recognise the decisive moment and will advise action then?

BURKE: The law officers of the Crown. Trust us.

GOVERNOR: Very well, Mr Burke; but be it on your heads.

There is sound of a disturbance off. BEDWARD's voice is heard offstage.

BEDWARD: I want to see the Governor.

GUARD: I'm sorry. The Governor is in a conference.

BEDWARD: I must see the Governor.

DAWSON: *(Terrified.)* It's him…Bishop Bedward. I don't want him to find me here.

BEDWARD bursts in, pursued by GUARD.

BEDWARD: I demand the right to see the Governor.

BURKE: You don't demand anything here, Sir.

BEDWARD: *(Seeing DAWSON.)* Ah, Pastor Dawson, so this is where you spend your afternoons. Moving in important circles, Pastor Dawson! *(Staring silently at each in turn.)* In very exalted company.

GOVERNOR: Now listen to me, Mr Bedward, our patience has worn thin with you. Don't press your luck with us any further.

BEDWARD: You speak of patience, Sir. Your police force have been trying the patience of my members. I come here today to warn that my people in Union Camp are not going to put up with any more police harassment and brutality.

GOVERNOR: They will obey the authority of the state.

BEDWARD: The only authority we obey is the authority of God.

BURKE: Let's get something straight, Mr Bedward. Are you threatening at King's House, in open defiance of His Excellency the Governor, to break the law?

BEDWARD: I am not threatening anything. I am warning you to stop the war against poor black people.

GOVERNOR: And I am warning you, Mr Bedward, to confine yourself to religious matters, to keep politics out of religion, to forget questions of race, colour, class and politics, to show due respect and regard for constituted authority. Otherwise the power and influence that you have achieved for yourself within the Church, and on which you now seek to build your wild fantasies of empire, will be swept away from under you by the superior power of the state. Go back to August Town with that message and never dare cross this threshold again unless commanded by me to come.

BEDWARD still stares at GOVERNOR. CONGREGATION sing 'Don't You Trouble Shepherd'.

SCENE X

Union Camp. BEDWARD and DAWSON discovered.

BEDWARD: So your friends at King's House want to test my power, Dawson, with their little authority of state. Don't they know who I am? They don't realise that I am God?

DAWSON: Shepherd!

BEDWARD: You don't realise it either.

DAWSON: Bishop! That's blasphemy. Stop now. You've gone too far.

BEDWARD: Better to be blasphemous than to be a house slave, Dawson.

DAWSON: Please, Bishop. For your own sake and for the sake of the Church…

BEDWARD: Pack up and go, Dawson. We have enough enemies outside Union Camp. We don't need any within.

DAWSON: *(Going.)* Oh, Shepherd, I'll pray for you.

HENRY approaches from opposite direction. DAWSON holds him.

Why don't you for once tell him not what he wants to hear but what's good for him and the Church?

DAWSON goes. A bewildered HENRY approaches BEDWARD.

BEDWARD: Oh, Pastor Henry, it's a great comfort to know that I can depend on your loyalty.

HENRY: Thank you, Shepherd.

BEDWARD: Dawson's treachery has been a great shock to me, Pastor Henry.

HENRY: I know, Shepherd.

BEDWARD: Dawson is excommunicated from the Church. His place will be taken, as from now, by Elder Steele.

HENRY: A very good choice, Shepherd.

BEDWARD: I have just had a vision, Henry…the greatest vision of all.

HENRY: Yes, Shepherd.

BEDWARD: In this vision, Henry, I came face to face with God, and God said to me, 'Who do you say that you are?' And I answered, 'Why? I am Alexander Bedward.' And God the Father said unto me. 'You are Alexander Bedward to men. But you are my messenger on earth. And they that follow you will know that you are a part of the Holy Trinity. You are Jesus Christ come again to redeem the sins of the world. And you are the Holy Ghost the Comforter.'

HENRY: Yes, Shepherd.

BEDWARD: You hear me, Henry? In the vision God told me I am Jesus Christ and the Holy Ghost… Redeemer and Comforter.

HENRY: Amen.

BEDWARD: You don't seem surprised, Henry.

HENRY: I have always known it, Shepherd.

BEDWARD: You are a man of remarkable understanding, Henry.

HENRY: Thank you, my Lord and Master!

BEDWARD: That sounds good, Henry. Lord and Master!

HENRY: Not only good, Lord, but right too.

BEDWARD: Henry, you will sit on the right hand of God. Call the people. Let me tell them about the wonderful visitation of the Father unto the Son and Holy Ghost.

HENRY: Yes, my Lord and Master. *(HENRY goes. MRS BEDWARD enters. Mean looks are exchanged between them.)*

MRS BED: Alexander…

BEDWARD: Say 'Lord and Master'.

MRS BED: You are blaspheming.

BEDWARD: You blaspheme, Woman. How dare you enter into the presence of the most high to speak with such disrespect?

MRS BED: I am still your wife.

BEDWARD: Speak not to me of worldly matters. I am here about my father's business.

MRS BED: You're not well. You must go and see the doctor.

BEDWARD: Doctor? You want me to see a doctor? I, who have cured the incurable? I, who doctors envy, hate and vilify, must see a doctor? Begone, Jezebel!

MRS BED: Alexander...

BEDWARD: Lord and Master. I am your Lord and Master.

MRS BED: Please, for God's sake. Be sensible.

BEDWARD: For God's sake is for my sake, Woman. I am God.

MRS BED: Stop now before it's too late.

BEDWARD: Repent, Woman. You are about to be cast into outer darkness. You have no faith, and time is running out for those who are lacking in faith.

MRS BED: Alexander.

BEDWARD: Begone. I must talk to my people. The hour of destiny is at hand.

MRS BEDWARD goes. CONGREGATION gather, led by HENRY and STEELE singing 'Onward Christian Soldiers' – all but the last verse.

BEDWARD: Brothers and Sisters, all white rascals shall perish! White and black rascals shall perish. The enemy are at hand, but the soldiers of the cross are ready to meet the threat of the forces of darkness. It was the same with Paul Bogle in Morant Bay. It's the same with Marcus Garvey today. See the pages of the Daily Gleaner how they revile Garvey? Every man who speaks on behalf of the poor black people of this country is a target for attack from the white sepulchre. Cain was a white man, and Cain is still doing his work; but I, Alexander Bedward, have comeas a black man to save the black race.

CONGREGATION, led by SARAH, shout approval.

HENRY: *(Singing.)* Onward, Christian Soldiers...

CONGREGATION all join in singing last verse of 'Onward Christian Soldiers'.

BEDWARD: The Lord is ready to release the plagues and let them descend upon mankind with a vengeance.

ALL: Hallelujah.

BEDWARD: Adam, the first man, sinned against God, and
God's wrath was stirred against Adam…and every
man thereafter was born with Adam's sin… And
God, forgiving, sent his son to redeem the sins of the
world… But they mocked him, and jeered him,and
spat upon him… And God took away His son, and in
his great forgiveness promised to deliver unto man the
Holy Ghost… As Christianity succeeded Judaism, so
Bedwardism succeeded Christianity… The candle you
use in your vow service is like unto the divine trinity.
The tallow represents the Father, the wick is the Son,
which proceedeth from the Father, and the flame is the
Holy Ghost, the light of the world. I am wick and flame;
the Son and the Holy Ghost.

ALL: Glory! Amen!

BEDWARD: He that will humbly follow after me, take up his
cross and come, for, saith the Lord Almighty the Father:
'Alexander Bedward, thou art the Son and the Holy
Ghost, which I have sent to redeem the sins of the world.
And I am pleased with thee. Prepare thyself to fly into
the heavens, for I have need of thee. And take with thee
into the skies; yes into the skies, whatever of thy disciples
will willingly take up the cross and follow thee; for I shall
send down fire to rain upon the earth; yea, but three
days after thou art come into heaven.

Great handclapping, shouting, from the CONGREGATION.

BEDWARD: Therefore, on Christmas Eve, 1920, I shall ascend
to my Father. I shall fly away into the skies.

SARAH: Fly!

ALL: Fly! Fly! Fly! *(Great jubilation.)*

BEDWARD: Three days later, I shall return for such of my
people as are found in Union Camp; and we shall all
soar into the blue beyond together… But on the 30th day
of December, 1920, the Lord will send down his fire to
scorch the earth, to destroy cities, countries, continents

and all mankind. So woe unto any sinner who is found wanting.

Tremendous rejoicing... The CONGREGATION sing: 'We Shall Have A Grand Time Up In Heaven'.

End of Act One.

ACT TWO

SCENE I

Union Camp. The CONGREGATION sing 'I am Coming Home.' The CONGREGATION hums. MRS BEDWARD approaches BEDWARD.

MRS BED: Alexander.

BEDWARD: What do you want?

MRS BED: I want you to do the only sensible thing you can do now. Tell the people that you will not ascend to heaven.

BEDWARD: What is this to do with you?

MRS BED: Alexander, people are continuing to pour into the Camp. More people are selling out their possessions at your command. Show courage and let it be known now that there will be no ascension.

BEDWARD: Who said there will be no ascension? And how dare you question God's plan?

MRS BED: Many people's lives depend on you, Alexander... even little children who cannot help themselves.

BEDWARD: I must go to my Father. I must fly away to glory.

MRS BED: But, my dear, Alexander, you cannot.

BEDWARD: I am not your dear Alexander. I am your Lord and Master.

MRS BED: You postponed your ascension from Christmas Eve to New Year's Eve. Save further suffering by announcing once and for all that the ascension is cancelled...not postponed.

BEDWARD: You are an angel of darkness come to interrupt the Lord's work. It cannot be. The Lord my Father has called me, and I must go to Him.

MRS BED: No man has ever flown; remember that.

BEDWARD: If a man has enough faith he can fly like the birds; and in any case I am not a man.

MRS BED: You have fathered three children by me.

BEDWARD: You reduce everything to flesh. You are Eve, Jezebel, Delilah and Sapphira. You are the scarlet woman. Go, before I lose my temper *(In a rage.)* Call me Henry. I want Henry.

MRS BEDWARD goes. CONGREGATION starts singing 'Fly Away Home', INSPECTOR GENERAL enters, talks to INSPECTOR on the fringe of the crowd.

INSP. GEN: How's the situation, Inspector?

INSPECTOR: As quiet as one could expect in the circumstances, Sir.

INSP. GEN: We'll maintain our hourly check from headquarters, but if you find matters getting out of hand contact us immediately for reinforcements.

INSPECTOR: Don't you think it's time we took in Bedward, Sir?

INSP. GEN: The Governor and the Attorney General have asked that we move carefully in this case. We are to consult the Attorney General before arresting Bedward… unless there is an outbreak of disorder or a serious breach of the peace.

INSPECTOR: I do feel though, Sit, that this farce has gone on long enough.

INSP. GEN: Don't worry, Inspector, I believe the end is nigh for Lord Bedward. He has put his own neck in the noose and today could be his day of reckoning.

INSPECTOR GENERAL goes. HENRY approaches BEDWARD.

BEDWARD: Henry, you do believe, don't you, that I can ascend to my Father? And send fire to rain down on earth?

HENRY: Yes, Lord. Why?

BEDWARD: But suppose I am not prepared when the time is come, Henry?

HENRY: How, Lord?

BEDWARD: Don't call me 'Lord', Henry. Call me 'Shepherd'. I am your Shepherd.

HENRY: What's the problem, Shepherd?

BEDWARD: I'm not sure, Henry. I don't feel the strength that I should have at this time.

HENRY: You're going to ascend though, Shepherd.

BEDWARD: I believe so, Henry, but I wonder if anything could possibly go wrong.

HENRY: Why, Shepherd? Nothing could possibly go wrong. Look. Six thousand people have already come to Union Camp to ascend with you. And more coming over the hill.

BEDWARD: Six thousand people have sold out all their belongings, Henry, to fly with me... Some of them little children.

HENRY: Shepherd!

BEDWARD: Listen to those people singing, Henry. Listen to the spirit. If I don't make it, how am I going to live it down?

HENRY: If you don't make it, Shepherd? But you must.

BEDWARD: I have been a good man, Henry.

HENRY: Man, Shepherd?

BEDWARD: Say something to them, Henry.

HENRY: Look, Shepherd! A cloud passing overhead. Remember, Shepherd. It's the angels in that cloud...the angels waiting to welcome you home.

HAMILTON: *(To SARAH.)* Sister Plunkett, suppose the Lord and master don't ascend toady. Is what going happen?

SARAH: You doubt, Sister Hamilton.

HAMILTON: No, no. Not a matter of doubting, but just suppose.

SARAH: You are backsliding.

HAMILTON: Oh, Sister Plunkett, I not backsliding, but you must remember he postponed the ascension once before, so it could happen again.

SARAH: You are forgetting how you had a serious affliction, Sister Hamilton, and our Lord and Master cured you of it in his healing stream.

HAMILTON: I am not forgetting anything, Sister Plunkett. I just saying suppose the Lord had to postpone the ascension once more, what would happen?

SARAH: That is a serious sin you just committed, Sister Hamilton. You should bow down on your knees and beg forgiveness of our Lord and Master before it's too late. Take care that when we are taken up into the heavens with him you are not left back here to be scorched with fire.

HAMILTON goes down on her knees, in silent prayer, STEELE approaches BEDWARD. He carries a newspaper.

STEELE: You seen the editorial in the *Gleaner*, Shepherd?

BEDWARD: No, Steele. What do they have to say?

STEELE: It's the usual thing, Lord. The police should arrest the Shepherd.

BEDWARD: Read it to me, Steele.

STEELE: I don't think you would want to hear it, Lord. It's very bad.

BEDWARD: No. Read, Steele. Let me see the enemy out in the open so I can deal with him.

STEELE: *(Reading.)* 'It is against the law of this land for anyone to claim that he possesses supernatural powers or is able to foretell the future and we know of no good reason why Mr Bedward of August Town should enjoy immunity…'

BEDWARD: The rats!

STEELE: 'When he announces that on a certain day he will ascend to Heaven, he is claiming to be able to foretell the future. When he declares that he will be translated while alive, and when he predicts destruction of cities or other happenings of a similar kind, he arrogates to himself supernatural characteristics and powers.'

BEDWARD: And have I not been healing people for thirty years?

STEELE: 'There is in Jamaica no question of non-interference with native religions.'

BEDWARD: They are not serious.

STEELE: 'We have no native religions.'

BEDWARD: Oh.

STEELE: 'The recognised religions of this country are the religions of Europe; we are not here concerned to maintain "native customs"; the whole aim of our institutions in the last three centuries has been to root out all "native customs" entirely.'

BEDWARD: Ah hah! They've admitted it. Now it's there for all the world to see.

STEELE: 'After Friday, then, if these August Town demonstrations continue, we hope the police will move to have decency observed at August Town, and to compel Mr Bedward to cease his wild predictions.'

HENRY: Ah, Shepherd, they have not read Psalm Sixty-eight, verse thirty-one: 'Princes shall come out of Egypt; Ethiopia shall soon stretch out her hands unto God.'

BEDWARD: You see the wickedness in them, Henry? Where were they in all the hundreds of years of colonial rule that people in this country have suffered from poverty? Where have their voices been since the time of Columbus? And what of those who come to Union Camp and are clothed and fed by us? Why don't they tell the people that nobody leaves Union Camp in hunger?

HENRY: Let fire rain down upon their heads, Lord and Master. Burn! Burn!

BEDWARD: *(To STEELE.)* Why did you bring these poisonous words to me? Whose side are you on, Steele? Mine or my enemies?

STEELE: But, Shepherd...

HENRY: *(Almost involutarily.)* No 'but' don't come into it, man.

BEDWARD: Begone, Steele. Out of my sight. You are a messenger come from the Devil. You are a second Dawson.

STEELE: Lord, you can't believe that.

BEDWARD: You heard me? Out of my sight, Judas.

STEELE goes.

BEDWARD: Don't you forsake me, Henry.

HENRY: Never, Shepherd.

CONGREGATION stop humming.

BEDWARD: Why have they stopped singing, Henry? Tell them to continue the song.

HENRY: It is ten o'clock, Shepherd...it is time for you to fly to your Father.

BEDWARD: Ten o'clock? But the time has passed so quickly. I don't think I'm ready. Henry. I can't go yet.

HENRY: I believe you can, Shepherd.

BEDWARD: Talk to them, Henry. Tell them the time's not yet at hand.

HENRY: I can't talk to them, Shepherd. It's you they're looking to.

BEDWARD: *(Boldly, having risen.)* Thus saith the Lord God Almighty to me,

'Alexander Bedward, stay with your sheep for two more hours and ascend thou at 12 noon.' *(As he sits, weakly to himself.)* My God, my God, why hast thou forsaken me?

HENRY: Pray, Shepherd...you will do it.

BEDWARD: Quiet, Henry... Listen to them, Henry... What are they muttering about? They're saying I let them down, Henry... Listen to them.

(Disappointed chatter. CONGREGATION sing, then hum 'Down In The Valley'.)

BEDWARD: They're looking this way, Henry...straight at me the six thousand of them are looking.

HENRY: It's twelve o'clock, Shepherd... You are going to do it aren't you, Shepherd?

CONGREGATION stop singing abruptly.

BEDWARD: Thus saith the Lord God Almighty to me: 'Alexander Bedward, put off your flight until 3 p.m.' *(Sitting weakly.)* O, my Father, if it be possible, let this cup pass from me.

More chatter from CONGREGATION. 'Down in the Valley' picks up again, not quite so spirited. CONGREGATION stop singing abruptly.

BEDWARD: Thus saith the Lord God Almighty: Alexander Bedward, the time is still not ripe... You will ascend to your Father at 10 p.m.'

Impatient murmur from CONGREGATION, then a dispirited start to the hymn... Sound of crickets and treefrogs. Once more the CONGREGATION stop singing with a hushing.

BEDWARD: Thus saith the Lord God Almighty to me: 'Alexander Bedward, if you ascend tonight, your people will be like sheep without a shepherd... Therefore, I have ordained that you remain on earth, yea, seventeen more years... Lead your people.

CONGREGATION say a great involuntary 'Oh, no!'.

BEDWARD: It is finished.

HENRY: I'm sorry, Shepherd.

BEDWARD: Don't talk to me now, Henry... Please.

HENRY: You'd better take a rest, Shepherd.

BEDWARD: Yes. Please see that I am not disturbed... I can't see anybody tonight.

BEDWARD exits.

HENRY: Goodnight, Shepherd.

BEDWARD makes no reply. The CONGREGATION sing very sadly: 'Bright Soul, Whe' Mek You Tun' Back?' Lights dim out. Song ends.

SCENE II

Union Camp. HENRY and STEELE are discovered.

HENRY: Pastor Steele, the Shepherd wants to see you.

STEELE: About what? I suppose he's going to put me out of the Church for reading a newspaper editorial that he asked me to read.

HENRY: How you so touchy of late, Steele? All I said is that the Shepherd want to see you.

STEELE: Somebody turn his mind against me. Somebody say something to him about me, and I have a pretty damn good idea who it would be. *(Suspiciously.)* By the way, Henry, how much money the Church have now?

HENRY: Don't ask me. I don't know.

STEELE: You don't know? Then who keeps the money?

HENRY: If you want to know, ask the Shepherd. I report to him only. Any, anyway, what's your interest in the finances of the Church?

STEELE: It is my Church. I have worked as hard as any man to acquire whatever we have acquired. That's my interest.

HENRY: *(Sarcastically.)* I beg your pardon! Remember the Shepherd want to see you. Don't keep him waiting.

STEELE goes toward BEDWARD. SARAH approaches HENRY.

SARAH: Good evening, Pastor Henry.

HENRY: Good evening, Sister Plunkett. Still keeping the faith, Sister.

SARAH: Yes, Pastor Henry. Some backslide. Some waver. Some question. Some doubt. But not I. I shall remain faithful forever.

HENRY: Good, Sister. Good. Good. Somehow we must keep God's children together. Help me round up the flock for the prayer meeting, Sister Plunkett.

SARAH: Yes, Pastor.

HENRY and SARAH exit.

BEDWARD: You have been staying away from me, Pastor Steele. What's the matter?

STEELE: Nothing, Shepherd.

BEDWARD: Remember, Steele, we have a great struggle ahead of us. We all must stay together for the battle.

STEELE: Of course, Shepherd.

BEDWARD: I alone can't carry out the work.

STEELE: Yes, Shepherd. You have my support as long as God continue to breathe the breath of life in me, Shepherd.

BEDWARD: Thank you, Pastor Steele. That's a great comfort to me.

The CONGREGATION led by HENRY, enter singing, 'If I Had The Wings Of A Dove'. Its tempo increases steadily. The last few notes are dragged, as the CONGREGATION are spent.

BEDWARD: Yes, my children! Never mind what Satan say… Dance and sing and make merry.

General approval from CONGREGATION.

BEDWARD: What a struggle we have to put up against the forces of evil.

CONGREGATION moan assent.

BEDWARD: But it can't last forever, Children… The ram is going to start bucking! And, woe be unto his enemies!

ALL: Amen.

BEDWARD: Woe unto any man who forces me to lift this rod… The stinking newspaper writers who won't leave mi name alone, the thieving doctors and parsons who keep making complaints against me to the Police with their damned lies…Look at today's paper for instance…Any of you see today's paper?

Mixed reply from the CONGREGATION.

BEDWARD: Today's paper is like all the rest… The Police should arrest Bedward, they say. But I warning them. The war is on… The Lord is rising up against his enemies!

WOMAN runs onstage, accosts SARAH, who has a pumpkin in hand.

WOMAN: I want back mi pumpkin. You hear what I say? I want back mi pumpkin!

BEDWARD: *(Masterfully.)* Woman… How dare you come into Union Camp to disturb the Lord's counsel?

WOMAN: One of you member go through mi barb wire fence and tief mi pumpkin. I want it back, or the two of we going work house tonight.

BEDWARD: Shu…Shu…Shu! You can't come in here with that kind of talk…Not in here.

WOMAN: I in here already.

BEDWARD: Well, out you go!

WOMAN: I want justice first… Just give mi mi pumpkin.

WOMAN grabs, but SARAH holds fast. There is a tussle with the pumpkin between the two.

WOMAN: Give mi mi pumkin… You stinking tief, you!

SARAH: Over mi dead body... Is who-fa pumpkin?

WOMAN: Is my own... Is outa my garden you tek it from.

SARAH: You have any mark on it? Eh, Jezebel?

BEDWARD brings his stick down on the strange woman's half of the pumpkin... She releases her hold in time. HENRY closes in and gently relieves SARAH of it. BEDWARD turns on the WOMAN.

BEDWARD: Now, you go back through the gate this minute... And I don't want to see your face in here again. You lucky you's a woman, or I would make your hide pay for this today.

WOMAN: Is all right... Cook mi pumpkin and eat it... Give a slice to each of them... And come back. You hear, mi love? I going inject the vine with poison for you... Come back.

BEDWARD: All right, enough from you. Don't let me use mi rod, Sister.

BEDWARD pushes out the WOMAN.

WOMAN: *(Off.)* Oonoo dutty stinking set of tief, oonoo!

A handful of MEMBERS go after her, but bump into the CENSUS ENUMERATOR, who is quite bewildered.

BEDWARD: Who you?... And what you want?

ENUMER: I am the Census Enumerator collecting information in this area.

BEDWARD: Outside with you and your confounded papers.

ENUMER: You didn't seem to hear me, Mr Bedward...I am...

BEDWARD: I don't care who you are... Outside... Outside!

BEDWARD strikes the ENUMERATOR repeatedly with his stick. ENUMERATOR flees. Almost immediately JABEZ PLUNKETT enters.

BEDWARD: Eh! What is this now?

PLUNKETT: I come for my wife... Name of Sarah Plunkett... I hear she in the Church here.

BEDWARD: You mistaken, Mr Plunkett... Your wife is not here.

PLUNKETT: Then is who that? Sarah, what you leave mi house for? Thirty years now we married and you and me never have one thing and you just suddenly ups and leave mi house? Is what come over you, Woman?

BEDWARD: You making a mistake, Brother... This woman is not your wife.

PLUNKETT: Who you to be telling me who is mi wife and who is not?

BEDWARD: She is my wife, Brother.

CONGREGATION laugh.

PLUNKETT: Your wife? Sarah, you mean to say...

BEDWARD: Take a look at the sisters... They are all my wives... Every one of them.

ALL SISTERS step forward, curtsey. More laughter from CONGREGATION.

PLUNKETT: Sarah, you going stand up there and allow the man to say a thing like that and you don't prove to him who is your lawful husband?

SARAH: I sorry, Jabez, but I had to leave you... You can't serve two masters, Jabez.

BEDWARD: *(Weightily.)* Well said, Sister Plunkett... You hear that, Brother? You can't serve two masters... It got to be God or mammon... You can't serve two masters.

The CONGREGATION pick up the chant – 'You can't serve two masters'... PLUNKETT exits. Enter a POLICE SERGEANT and a DISTRICT CONSTABLE.

SERGT: All right! Enough nonsense go on in this place now. Where the woman with the pumpkin?

BEDWARD: What you want now? Look here, boy, mind you own damn business.

SERGT: Do you realise it's an officer of the Law you're talking to?

BEDWARD: To hell with the Law!

SERGT: *(Advancing on him.)* No, no, no...

> *CONGREGATION surround the POLICEMEN, throw them to the ground.*

BEDWARD: *(Having taken off POLICEMAN's hat.)* Who-fa crown this?

SERGT: Is King George's hat, you see?

BEDWARD: *(Scornfully.)* King George of England. Tell King George of England that King Bedward of Jamaica throw away King George crown *(Tossing hat off.)* and flog King George house slave.

> *BEDWARD hits POLICEMEN with rod. POLICEMEN flee as MOB shout first 'Lick them' and then 'Hold them'.*

BEDWARD: They are going to send a bigger fish to come here and ask questions... Nobody answer a word... Just sing and dance.

> *HENRY starts the song 'Fly Away Home'.*

> *INSPECTOR and SGT MAJOR enter unobtrusively.*

BEDWARD: See, Children? What did I tell you? We have to rise up and do battle against our enemies. They have been oppressing us for too long, and the Lord has told me as His Son to go to Kingston to deliver His people... I am going to Kingston for that purpose tomorrow morning. At the crack of dawn, I'm marching into the city for a manifestation. You are prepared to go?

ALL: Yes, my Lord!

INSPECTOR: Come, Sergeant Major *(POLICEMEN walk over to BEDWARD.)* Listen, Mr Bedward. Don't make things difficult for yourself. Stay in August Town and don't talk nonsense about marching into the city.

BEDWARD: But I must go. I must obey my Father. Do you know who I am? I am the Lord Jesus Christ.

INSPECTOR: I know all that, but...

BEDWARD: You know it? Then tell me; must I obey you and disobey the command of my Father?

INSPECTOR: I'm only here to tell you, Mr Bedward, not to attempt any march. It's against the law.

BEDWARD: It is no good asking me not to go... I must take them out tomorrow. You can shoot me if you like, but I shall march. We shall march.

SARAH: *(Singing.)* But I hear the word of the Shepherd say...

ALL: Babylon, your throne gone down, gone down;

Babylon, you throne gone down *(Then chanting.)* March! March! March! March!

INSPECTOR: Listen to me, Mr Bedward...

HENRY starts 'Onward Christian Soldiers' to frustrate the INSPECTOR's attempt to convince BEDWARD. The move succeeds INSPECTOR signals the SGT MAJOR to leave. They exit.

CONGREGATION sing 'Onward, Christian Soldiers' on march.

SCENE III

Mona Road, early morning.

SGT MAJOR: I thought you said, Inspector, that the Governor was sending the military to help us.

INSPECTOR: Don't worry, Sergeant Major, they're observing the situation close at hand and will come to our help if necessary.

BEDWARD's FLOCK are heard approaching, singing 'Onward Christian Soldiers'.

INSPECTOR: Down, everybody... Here they come.

The procession appears, headed by BEDWARD. HENRY and STEELE are close behind, and following them a banner on white cloth spanned by two poles with the following inscription in black: 'The Jamaica Native Baptist Free Church. A Bedward, Shepherd.' A verse of scripture follows... Behind the banner are several smaller ones... The five ELDERS carry white painted wooden swords. Each member of the procession bears a little white cross. Some of the women wave palm leaves. As the police and military close round them, BEDWARD falls to his knees. The procession comes to a halt.

BEDWARD: Eli, Eli! What is this?

INSPECTOR: You're not moving a step further.

MARCHERS freeze as the guns become more alert.

INSPECTOR: Sergeant Major…

SGT MAJOR: Yes, Sir.

SGT MAJOR goes to INSPECTOR. They exchange a few secret words. MARCHERS mark time singing 'Onward Christian Soldiers'.

INSPECTOR: So you want to march to Kingston.

ALL: Yes, Satan.

INSPECTOR: All right. But I'm warning you. It would be better for you to go back to August Town.

The procession starts, but with the FORCES flanking them, single file… They sing 'Onward Christian Soldiers'.

SCENE IV

Courtroom. SAM BURKE presides, in military uniform. There are several policemen on duty. DELEON, DEPUTY CLERK OF COURTS, prosecuting.

DELEON: *(Aside, to INSPECTOR.)* If they planned to march into Kingston, Inspector, how on earth did you get them into Half Way Tree courthouse?

INSPECTOR: We simply marched our forces, single file, on either side of them and piloted them into the courtyard here. Then we locked the gate behind them. Once they insisted on the march they never had a chance. I warned them, but the poor fools wouldn't listen.

BURKE: *(Gavelling.)* Put Alexander Bedward in the dock.

CROWD, off, sing 'Don't You Trouble Shepherd'. BEDWARD enters, escorted by a SERGEANT and a CORPORAL with rifles.

BURKE: *(To POLICEMEN.)* You two may go. *(POLICEMEN bow, exit.)* Hold on a moment. Will someone tell those people to stop that noise immediately.

A POL'MAN: Shut up.

There is silence. BEDWARD walks to the side bar, removes his white cap.

BURKE: What is this man charged with?

DELEON: Assaulting a constable in the execution of his duty.

BURKE: You heard the charge... How do you plead? Guilty or not guilty?

BEDWARD makes no reply: stares at BURKE.

BURKE: For the second time... Are you pleading guilty or not guilty?

Still no answer; still staring.

DELEON: Under such circumstances, won't Your Honour remand him for medical observation?

BURKE: I am going to remand you for medical observation for a week.

No reply; no gesture; stony stare.

BURKE: Remand him in custody until next Wednesday.

BEDWARD is removed.

BURKE: Next case.

SCENE V

Half Way Tree lockup. BEDWARD sits on a bed, behind bars. MRS BEDWARD stands at the bars, visiting.

MRS BED: Alexander, I've got permission from the authorities to bring you a comfortable mattress. Is there anything else you want me to get for you?

BEDWARD: No. You have done more than enough. Perhaps more than I deserve. Thank you very much. But tell me; what have they done to my people?

MRS BED: The elders were given two months at hard labour. More than two hundred of the other men were given fourteen days at hard labour. The men were sent to Spanish Town prison. Fifty of the women were tried and sentenced to seven days hard labour at the General Penitentiary. The judge warned the other women and let them go without a trial.

BEDWARD: And what kind of justice is that that is not equal for one and all?

MRS BED: Questions were asked in the Legislative Council. Some of the members felt it was unfair for the judge to try and sentence nearly three hundred people in three hours. The Governor pardoned all the people who were sentenced, so they are now free.

BEDWARD: How have our children stood up to all this?

MRS BED: You can be proud of them. They have been very strong.

BEDWARD: And what about the people at August Town? Are they still faithful?

MRS BED: Some of them. Most have left the Camp. They were disappointed. Their spirit was broken.

BEDWARD: That was what the Scribes and Pharisees ordained. They will not rest until they have separated me from my flock. But, I am not finished. Oh, no… Did you bring the *Gleaner*?

MRS BED: Yes.

BEDWARD: What the editorial say? Read it to me.

MRS BED: You sure you want to hear it? It's very bad.

BEDWARD: It can't make matters worse than they are. Please read it.

MRS BED: *(Reading.)* 'If Bedwardism is a religion to be respected, the sooner the very name of God is forgotten in Jamaica the better!'

BEDWARD: What blasphemous pagans they are.

MRS BED: 'Those who are now disposed to assert that the peaceful pilgrimage of the Bedwardites towards Kingston should have been regarded merely as the march of a body of Salvationists through this city are evidently in ignorance of the vile orgies that have taken place at August Town, of the shameless obscenity that has disgraced that now infamous place.'

BEDWARD: What crime did we commit except that we were poor and black? Eh? I didn't cause the white man's church to turn away the black people. It was the white man's church that turned them away. I only received them and gave them a religion they could understand and believe in. And in return I was given their loyalty and their love.

MRS BED: Are you sure you want me to continue?

BEDWARD: Yes… Yes. Go on.

MRS BED: 'Since when has West Africa superseded Palestine? Even to suggest that it has done so is to insult the decency and intelligence of the vast majority of our people, who have never been Bedwardites and who are now determined that the August Town orgies must cease.'

BEDWARD: They keep on writing about orgies. If they consider worship an orgy, no wonder they are so ungodly.

MRS BED: 'We are glad that the Bedwardites were stopped before any harm was done; and we hope that the August Town demonstrations are over.'

BEDWARD: Yes, of course. That's what they want. But it won't happen. Not while I'm alive. Not even after I'm gone from this earth.

MRS BED: 'If they are not, we shall call upon the Government to deal with them effectively once and for all. For this disgrace to Jamaica has lasted long enough. We must choose now between tolerating West African survivals on

a gigantic scale and preserving the name of Jamaica as a
country civilised.'

BEDWARD: And they call that fair play – an editorial like that
while I'm on remand and two days before I am due for
trial! Their judgement will be a terrible one.

SARAH PLUNKETT arrives with newspaper and food carrier.

SCENE VI

*Half Way Tree court: MR SAM BURKE presiding. INSPECTOR WRIGHT
prosecuting. BEDWARD stands in dock.*

BURKE: Alexander Bedward, you are clearly a person of
unsound mind and therefore not responsible for your
actions. You may go.

*BEDWARD walks out of the dock into the road. The SPECTATORS
jubilantly sing 'Come We Blow The Note'. SERGEANT MAJOR and
the other policemen bundle BEDWARD back into court.*

SARAH: Oonu try him already and find him not guilty.

SPECTATORS are agitated.

BURKE: *(Gavelling.)* Silence. When you come to my court you
obey the rules of the court or you will be made to pay
the price of your disobedience.

BEDWARD is placed in the dock.

HAMILTON: Boy, when the law out to get you, there's no
escape.

SARAH: *(Loudly.)* They can do nothing to the Shepherd. If
they try him a thousand times him win them a thousand
times.

CROWD: Yes. Tell them.

BURKE: We'll soon see about that…Inspector Wright.

INSPECTOR: Alexander Bedward, you are charged that, being
a person of unsound mind, you were found wandering at
large. How do you plead? Guilty or not guilty?

BEDWARD: I have been doing evangelistic work for thirty-three years and five months.

INSPECTOR: Call Dr John Edwards.

POL'MAN: Dr John Edwards.

DR EDWARDS takes witness stand, CONSTABLE hands him Bible.

CONSTAB: I swear by Almighty God…

EDWARDS: I swear by Almighty God…

CONSTAB: That the evidence I shall give in this case…

EDWARDS: That the evidence I shall give in this case…

CONSTAB: Shall be the truth…

EDWARDS: Shall be the truth…

CONSTAB: The whole truth…

EDWARDS: The whole truth…

CONSTAB: And nothing but the truth…

EDWARDS: And nothing but the truth…

INSPECTOR: Will you state your name, please?

EDWARDS: Dr John Edwards.

INSPECTOR: And your occupation, Dr Edwards?

EDWARDS: I am District Medical Officer, St Andrew.

INSPECTOR: Do you know the accused, Alexander Bedward?

EDWARDS: Yes, Sir.

INSPECTOR: How long have you known him?

EDWARDS: One week.

BEDWARD: One week! Then you don't know me, boy.

CROWD: Tell them, Shepherd.

Uproar. BURKE gavels.

POL'MAN: Order in court!

BURKE: Now, listen here, you. Don't stretch my patience any further.

INSPECTOR: Dr Edwards, will you tell the court what you know about Alexander Bedward?

EDWARDS: I have had the accused, Alexander Bedward, under medical observation for one week now. I have had two long talks with him and I am satisfied that he is a person of unsound mind.

INSPECTOR: Have you consulted anyone else or referred his case to anyone else?

EDWARDS: Yes. I referred the case to Dr Denis Williams of the lunatic asylum.

INSPECTOR: Why did you consult Dr Williams?

EDWARDS: Because he is a psychiatrist of considerable experience.

INSPECTOR: And what was Dr Williams' opinion?

EDWARDS: The same as mine. His opinion is actually contained in a letter which I have here.

CONSTABLE takes letter; it is passed to MAGISTRATE.

INSPECTOR: Yes, Dr Edwards; why did you conclude that Alexander Bedward is of unsound mind?

EDWARDS: He suffers from hallucination of hearing. He believes that God speaks to him and tells him what to do. In addition, he is certainly dangerous. His hallucination is that He is Jesus Christ, that his mother was the Virgin Mary and that Joseph, the carpenter in the scriptures, was his step-father. He also professes to cure any disease by the water of the Hope River, which he claims he turned into medicine, and that those who use the water are cured of any malady. Those are his main delusions.

BURKE: I believe the defendant is the same person who said he was going to ascend to heaven on a certain day. He was going to fly.

COURT OFFICALS laugh.

SARAH: *(Rising.)* Order in court.

There is absolute silence. BURKE gives her a withering stare.

SARAH: *(Very properly.)* You must all follow the rules of His Majesty's Court.

BURKE: *(Severely.)* That is not your business. Sit.

(SARAH sits.)

BURKE: Proceed, Inspector.

INSPECTOR: I am through with the doctor, Sir.

BURKE: *(To BEDWARD.)* Do you wish to ask any questions of Dr Edwards before he leaves the stand?

No answer.

BURKE: Thank you, Dr Edwards. The Lord and Master of August Town has no questions for you.

DR EDWARDS leaves stand.

INSPECTOR: Call Sergeant Major Williams.

SERGEANT MAJOR WILLIAMS takes stand.

WILLIAMS: *(Taking Bible.)* I swear by Almighty God that the evidence I shall give in this case shall be the truth, the whole truth and nothing but the truth… Sergeant Major Williams of the Jamaica Constabulary Force.

INSPECTOR: Do you remember Wednesday the 27th of April, 1921?

WILLIAMS: Yes, Sir.

INSPECTOR: What happened on that day?

WILLIAMS: The defendant, Alexander Bedward, was leading a mob from August Town into Kingston. I escorted him to Half Way Tree station. He was brought before the court, but was remanded for medical observation.

INSPECTOR: Have you seen the defendant since that time?

WILLIAMS: Yes, Sir.

INSPECTOR: How often?

WILLIAMS: Twice a day.

INSPECTOR: Why?

A MAN: Police harassment!

BURKE gavels.

BURKE: Who said that? Who was that? Whoever you are you are treading on thin ice.

BEDWARD: *(In measured tone.)* We don't have ice on the ground in Jamaica.

FLOCK laugh. BURKE gavels. There is silence.

INSPECTOR: Yes, Sergeant Major. Why did you see the accused twice a day since he was remanded?

WILLIAMS: It's part of my duties to visit prisoners in the lock-up.

INSPECTOR: And what happened on your visits to the accused?

WILLIAMS: He talked freely with me. In the course of the conversation he kept on saying he was the Lord Jesus Christ, that August Town was the valley of Jehosophat and that those who wanted to be saved must go down to the valley.

He also said that the sea of Kingston would go as far as Up Park Camp by Mountain View Avenue; that there would be a tidal wave and only those who were at August Town would be saved. He also said that Cain was a white man, and he, Alexander Bedward, had come as a black man to save my race. And he said the end was now at hand.

BURKE: At least that wasn't far from the truth.

Officials laugh.

BURKE: Carry on.

WILLIAMS: On the night of Tuesday April 26, 1921, I accompanied Inspector Wright to August Town. We arrived at 6:30 p.m. There was a lot of shouting and clapping of hands, during which the accused, Bedward, said that the Lord had told him as His Son to go to Kingston to deliver his people, and he was going the next day. The Inspector pleaded with him not to go, but he replied; 'Do you know who I am? I am the Lord Jesus Christ. Must I obey you and disobey the command of my Father?' His members threatened violence and we had to withdraw.

INSPECTOR: And do you remember this morning, the 4th of May, 1921?

WILLIAMS: Yes, Sir. I saw the accused Alexander Bedward walking on Hagley Park Road, in front of the Half Way Tree courthouse. I thought it dangerous for him to be at large and I charged him on a warrant that being a person of unsound mind he was found wandering at large.

BURKE: *(To BEDWARD.)* Do you wish to ask any questions of Sergeant Major Williams?

No answer. WILLIAMS steps down.

HAMILTON: *(Sotto voce.)* Why the Shepherd don't cross-examine the witnesses?

SARAH: *(Sotto voce.)* No, Man. The Shepherd waiting to give him own evidence. That's when him going to blast them to pieces.

INSPECTOR: Your Honour, I could tell the same story as Sergeant Major Williams but I won't bore you.

BURKE: These stories are anything but boring, Inspector.

INSPECTOR: I shall call a number of witnesses who will tell stories of a series of atrocities in August Town, for example an overseer on the Mona property who will tell of the protection through violence given by the accused to church members who invaded and stole from the estate.

BEDWARD: Please give me fair play, Inspector.

SCENE VII

Half Way Tree Court.

BURKE: *(To BEDWARD.)* Stand.

VOICE: You can't talk to the Shepherd like that.

BURKE: This is my court, and I'll talk to any prisoner at the bar as I choose. Arrest that man.

POLICEMEN close in on the MAN. Pandemonium. BURKE gavels.

POL'MAN: Order in court.

POLICEMEN carry out MAN.

BURKE: *(Calling after them.)* Charge him with contempt of court. Alexander Bedward, stand.

BEDWARD stands.

BURKE: Alexander Bedward, having listened to all the evidence in this case…

BEDWARD: Can't I say something?

BURKE: Having listened to all the evidence in this case…

BEDWARD: Am I not allowed to speak?

BURKE: I find you guilty as charged…

VOICES: *(Severally.)* Unjust. Rubbish! What kind of judge is this?

BEDWARD: Can't I speak in my own defence?

BURKE: That being a person of unsound mind you were found wandering at large. I am committing you to the lunatic asylum.

BEDWARD: What kind of justice is this where I cannot even speak in my own defence?

BURKE: You heard the doctor's evidence. You are a person of unsound mind. A man of unsound mind is not responsible for his actions, his thoughts or his utterances. How can I therefore listen to you? You are a lunatic, Sir, and I cannot listen to any incoherent story. There is no room for more than one Messiah in our Christian island, and the true Messiah has long been taken from this earth. You are a danger not only to society but to civilisation itself. I have no doubt that if you commanded your people to jump into an inferno or to swallow poison, most of them would oblige.

BEDWARD: You use the force of the law, Judge, to suppress the people. The laws and institutions are made by the few to keep the many in subjugation. You may lock me away and stop the people from marching today, but your power is only temporary. No law, no judge, no newspaper and no governor can stop the people's march forever. When the people are ready to move, Judge, you and your soldiers, and your policemen and your Governor had better step aside, or you will be trampled underfoot.

BURKE: I understand you are very adept at quoting Holy Scripture. Have you ever tried St Matthew Chapter Twenty-four, Verse Twenty-four? 'For there shall arise false Christs, and false prophets, and shall show great signs and wonders; insomuch that, if it were possible, they shall deceive the very elect.' *(Looking at BEDWARD's followers.)* Anyone claiming to be the Messiah is either a rogue or a madman...or a mad rogue. He is a menace to peace and good order. We must protect the society from him. And we must protect him from himself. For, if we don't intervene, like the Pied Piper of Hamelin, he might lure the poor little rats to their deaths. Alexander Bedward, you are committed to the lunatic asylum. Take him away.

BEDWARD: *(To BURKE.)* There are my people. And there are thirty-three thousand more outside, one thousand for each year of my ministry. All of you in high places sought to destroy me because of the love they have for me. Well, you have succeeded to a point, because now you are using the brute force of the law to separate the Shepherd from his flock. But that separation is only temporary. There will come a time, Judge, when the brute force of the law will not be enough to stop the march of the people. When that day comes, Judge, we will roll over you, your Attorney General, your newspapers and your Governor. For that spiritual bond that unites me and my people you can never understand, much less enjoy.

You can put space between me and my people for the time being, Your Honour, but you will never win the battle for their souls. Brothers and Sisters, keep on singing. Sing until that day when we are ready to bring the Judge to his final judgement.

BURKE: *(To POLICEMEN.)* Take him away.

> *BEDWARD is removed. He is followed by procession of court officers. SPECTATORS sing 'Daniel, God surely will deliver'.*

> *End.*

DOWN IN THE VALLEY

I CAN HEAR THE SAVIOUR CALLING

LET DE POWER FALL ON ME

Oh, let de pow-er fall an me shep-herd. Let de pow-er fall an me. Oh, let de

pow-er fall an me shep - herd. Let de pow-er fall an me

DON'T YOU TROUBLE SHEPHERD

Don't you trou-ble shep-herd. Don't you trou-ble shep-herd.

For shep-herd have a key to o-pen sin-ners' heart.

Don't you trou - ble shep - herd.

PRESS ALONG

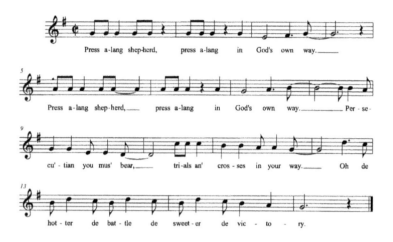

Press a-lang shep-herd, press a-lang in God's own way.

Press a-lang shep-herd, press a-lang in God's own way. Per-se-

cu'-tian you mus' bear, tri-als an' cros-ses in your way. Oh de

hot-ter de bat-tle de sweet-er de vic-to-ry.

FLY AWAY HOME TO GLORY

Fly a-way home to glo-ry, Fly a-way home.

Fly a-way home to glo-ry, Fly a-way home. One bright maw-nin'

when my work is o-ver I will fly a-way home.

BABYLON YUH THRONE GAWN DUNG

I can hear de voice of the shep-herd say, "Ba-by-lan yu throne gawn

dung, gawn dung. Ba - by-lan yu throne gawn dung."

ONWARD CHRISTIAN SOLDIERS

COME WE BLOW DE NOTE

BRIGHT SOUL

Bright soul_____ wha mek yu tun back? Bright soul_____ wha mek yu tun back? O bright soul_____ wha mek yu tun back? O yuh go - a Riv - er Jer - dan an' yuh tun back.

DANIEL GOD

Dan-iel God sure-ly will de-li - ver._____ Dan-iel God sure-ly will de-li - ver._____ If you on - ly look to him by faith __ Dan - iel God sure - ly will de - li - ver._____

THE CREATURES

BY CICELY WAITE-SMITH

Cicely Howland (1910-1978) born in Canada, educated in England and Switzerland, studied acting in Paris at the Atelier a drama school run by Charles Dullin. She acted with his company, with Jean Louis Barrault, and with Michel St. Denis. In London (1935) Cicely Howland acted in Obey's *Noah* with Sir John Gielgud under the direction of Michel St. Denis and seemed destined for a career in the English theatre when she married a Jamaican, Frank Waite-Smith and settled in Jamaica, where she directed *Sheridan's School for Scandal* for the Little Theatre Movement in 1942, wrote *Return to Paradise* (1950), *The Impossible Situation* (1960), *The Creatures*, a play in one act (1954), participated in a 1955 drama workshop organized by Knox College and the Extra Mural Dept. of the University College of the West Indies which devised *Sleepy Valley, Uncle Robert* (1957), *The Ravishers* (1957) and *African Slingshot* (1958). During her time in Jamaica she was involved in the country's march towards Independence and wrote articles for *Public Opinion* with the encouragement of Roger Mais among others. Her autobiography *The Long Run* (1961) was dedicated to Edna Manley, (sculptress, wife of Norman Washington Manley who was Chief Minister of Jamaica in 1955) a close friend and staunch admirer of her work. She eventually returned to England in 1960 and died there in 1978. She had one daughter Deirdre who lives in England.

First published in *Focus: an anthology of contemporary Jamaican writing* edited by Edna Manley, produced by the Extra Mural Department of The University College of the West Indies, 1956.

INTRODUCTION TO THE CREATURES
BY HONOR FORD-SMITH

*My Aunty Cicely was 'different' from the rest of us. They said she was English but I thought she looked Chinese because she had black hair and slanting eyes. Or perhaps it was her glamorous clothes or the fact that she spoke French and Italian and was an actress and had a daughter who had joined the circus. She was the only writer and actress that I knew personally and she lived in and wrote about Jamaica at a time when all the writers we studied were from Europe. And she didn't seem to care what people said about her. I'd catch the tail end of the talk as I came into the room: '...dunno how she could write that book! At least she used her maiden name.' One of the adults said. Then she saw me, and lowered her voice. I knew they were talking about **The Long Run** her book about her life, but I could never find a copy lying around to read.*

One Sunday afternoon in the 1950s I heard her familiar voice pouring out of the radio. She was reading a story. I don't remember the story itself; what I remember was being carried outside myself to some other space that was different than the everyday. I was there in the house on Hope Road but not there. When I caught myself I went and called everybody to listen. Only my mother came and she sat with me as I became aware for the first time that such activities constituted work and were not outside of the realm of everyday possibility. Or were they?

*Another afternoon, the play, **Return to Paradise** appeared unexpectedly on the television. Mitzi Townshend played Annie, a working-class Grandmother struggling to get back her job as a domestic servant in a home in upper St Andrew. Townsend played the battle to remain dignified in the face of class and racialized rejection with economy and grace. At the end the strength of character emerged from the understated way she expressed her anger in a brief mention of her grandson's drift into crime.*

This was the first drama about a Jamaican situation that I had ever seen and it only lasted 15 minutes. Everything else I had seen was either funny or a musical, or English. At the end the words: Written by Cicely Waite-Smith appeared in the credits. I'd never seen anything else that so carefully represented the casual brutality of Jamaica and its intimate consequences. How had she come to write something like that? I struggled to match the sensitivity of the characterization and the pathos of the piece to a world that seemed disinterested. Nobody at home or school talked to me openly about young boys going in and out of brothels as Annie did with Jean, the young woman she had helped raise. They all seemed to live such careful lives straining after an illusive, blinkered respectability.

Years later I met her after she moved to England. She was in her sixties still beautiful and elegant, living with her family in a small flat in Richmond surrounded by paintings from Jamaica. Johnny Lyon who used to sing falsetto at the UNIA concerts came round for lunch and then she took me to see a play at the Old Vic.

Cicely Howland/Waite-Smith was my Godmother and one of my mother's best friends. She was also married to an uncle of mine for a time. She officiated at my birth and my mother and I lived with her on Stanton Terrace for a time when I was a tiny baby. More important than that is the fact that her plays remain among a very few published Jamaican plays written by women before the 1960s. Howland was not Jamaican, at least not in the sense of being born or raised here. She was one of a number of white expatriate women who participated in the early anti-colonial nationalist cultural movements. Howland's main contribution was her prose and drama in Jamaica in the 1940s and 50s when she produced a series of stories and (mostly) one-act plays.

While her plays have importance as a historical record, what are we to make of them in the contemporary moment? How does her 'foreignness' and her 'whiteness' affect her representations of Jamaican society. Should we leave that out and pay attention only to the 'quality of the work' or should we try to understand what if anything it meant for her work?

Answering this question requires that we think of the theatre and more precisely her plays, as a public forum for the negotiation of ideas about community and belonging, as a way into the cultural narratives, symbols, and struggles of this time and that one. It requires that we think of the theatre as more than entertainment or the display of artistic skill. We need for example to remember that in a world where 80% of the globe was ruled by European colonial powers, the central problem of the 20th century was the problem of decolonization. That problem remains unsolved and its legacies are still with us. The fact was that when Howland wrote her plays, her social background as well as her skills enabled her to say what she said but it also affected how seriously what she said was taken in Jamaica. This was the result of historical inequity in her time: some people got to speak and be heard while the majority didn't and those who couldn't speak had to deal with the consequences of the way they were depicted by more powerful Others. My Aunt didn't choose her background but she did have to decide what use she would make of it, whether to accept the world the way it was or to try and change it.

It's commonplace to observe that one of the consequences of the colonial past is the idea that people who are different from us are either inferior or superior (to us) because of that difference – hence we speak about us and them/ or dem and wi. The colonizers, for example, imagined themselves as superior to those they governed and positioned these 'Others' as their opposites in all respects. We are rational. They are savage. We are good. They are evil, primitive/civilized; black/white; rational/irrational. In an effort to change this, nationalists struggling for freedom created new narratives or stories of community and identity. In so doing they often ended up reversing these binaries in the interest of the colonized.

One alternative to this constant repetition of opposites is to engage in dialogue across differences (such as those of race, class, gender and culture) and to do this while also questioning the power structures that create these differences in the first place. This approach is different than insisting on the idea that we are chosen and somehow better than everyone else while ignoring the powerful forces that make us the way we are. While much scholarship on the Caribbean focuses on racial tensions, Sara Abraham reminds us that it is the practice of multi-racialism in the context of Caribbean social movements that has much to teach. She proposes that when social movements begin to struggle for broad political goals, racialized groups begin to work together and racial barriers begin to come down.

Her most important point is that this challenge to the colonial and postcolonial status quo moves folks beyond the fixity of racial identities inherited from colonialism which is essential to the process of envisioning new social relations. (Abraham, 2007 pp. 91-100).

Abraham's important discussion of what a radical but inclusive multi-racialism might look like in the present and how we might envision equitable relations across racialized and gendered difference in a decolonized society is the starting point for this essay. I propose to read Waite-Smith's work as a site for the thinking about this issue. By teasing out some of the issues that emerge from her autobiography and her plays, I hope to name a few of the issues which we need to consider and negotiate if we are to envision an anti-colonial multi-racialism in a place that is also part of the African diaspora.

Beginnings

Cicely Howland was born in Canada to a well to do Anglo-Canadian family. She was educated in Europe and trained as an actress in England but it was her work as an actress at the celebrated Atelier Theatre in Paris in the 1920s that shaped her theatrical approach. Her approach to drama was far more French than English as *The Creatures* with its reliance on metaphor and mime attests. She worked at the Atelier under the direction of the actor Charles Dullin, a former student of Copeau, the influential French director. Copeau committed himself to building an art theatre based on principles of simplicity of style, freedom from overacting and careful textual interpretation. He taught his actors physical discipline, movement and improvisation. Dullin acted under Copeau and then began to teach and direct a generation of young actors, among them the legendary Antonin Artaud, Decroux and Marcel Marceau and Jean Louis Barrault who became Howland's friend and lover during the years at the Atelier. Howland performed in Obey's *Noah* and then joined a team of actors working with Michel St. Denis in the French countryside. She left the theatre for a short marriage and arrived in Jamaica after her divorce in the 1930s. These were the watershed years during which the anti-colonial struggle became redefined in terms of the nation state and independence.

The anticolonial movement, the Drumblair group and women in Jamaica

In Jamaica, Howland married Frank Waite-Smith, a Jamaican of mainly Portuguese Jewish extract and an early member of the People's National Party. She became close friends with Roger Mais and Edna Manley and was drawn into the Drumblair group, the informal artistic circle that formed around the Manleys. Drumblair, as their home was called, was a kind of anti-colonial 'salon' for mainly mixed-race middle-class artists, activists and intellectuals committed to the ideals of modernism, social progress and unity. There were few women in the circle and Edna Manley has emerged a towering figure – more or less the only woman to be noticed. She is credited with developing a nationalist aesthetic combining modernist impulses in European art to represent landscape and people in terms of archetypal images of prophetic and mythic potential.

But there were many other women active in the anti-colonial movement in the 1930s, 40s and 50s. Black women educated locally at Shortwood Teacher Training College offered significant leadership. In the early years these included educators such as Mary Morris Knibb, the first woman to be elected to the parochial board and Edith Dalton James an educator and PNP member. Amy Bailey led the fight for women's political rights and wrote for *Public Opinion* commenting on the racism endured by Black women and advocating for the professionalization of domestic work. Louise Bennett was not overtly political in a partisan sense but more than any other figure she created national narratives through her performances of Jamaican culture and her celebration of the Jamaican language and the wit of Black women.

Women who like Manley and Howland were white-skinned, were usually from elite families. Edith Clarke, the anthropologist and advocate for Jamaica Welfare and May Farqharson, feminist and birth control advocate were daughters of wealthy planters who atypically lived on the island. Waite-Smith was unlike them in that she could not claim Jamaican ancestry and her main contribution was through writing and in the rather less respectable field of drama. Like the mixed-race dancer Ivy Baxter, she worked in performance, though her plays did not appear until the 1950s when the thrust for self-government morphed into the short-lived attempt at regional federation.

Strangers, masking and the crisis of recognition

Howland's sense of the tenuousness and the strength of outsider status enters the narratives of her plays covertly. Her one-act play, *Africa Sling Shot*, is about an outsider who beguiles a rural village with tales of Africa and inspires them to imagine new possibilities. At one level the play is a didactic piece about the dangers of mob oratory and the value of British liberalism. At another level, it is a version of the stranger motif in literature. The stranger inspires while making the familiar strange, rather as Howland herself did. The trickster/storyteller though is not a hero. He turns out to be an escaped convict. When this is revealed the disillusioned community give up their dreams of overturning the social order, the stranger leaves and the status quo is re-established. The project of change fails because of the inauthenticity of the narrator and the sense of possibility inspired by the stranger exists only for a moment and then withers. The provocative but inspiring outsider can be read as a dramatic metaphor for Waite-Smith's life and work in Jamaica.

Her autobiography (1961) reveals all this even as it shocked the middle classes of upper St. Andrew. One *Gleaner* newspaper critic called it 'sordid' no doubt because of its explicit sexuality. In the book, Howland paints herself a perpetual outsider always in search of an authenticity that eludes her, just as her characters often fail at achieving their own subjectivity. In brief descriptions of her work in the theatre she explains that she comes closest to finding her own creativity when she assumes a mask. She writes:

> Now and then I acted again, including the part of Emily in Thornton Wilder's *Our Town*. I wrote earlier that in Canada I found in the theatre a release from myself. In a sense this was so, in another sense it is release into oneself that one finds, for it is easier to be oneself when one is someone else. (Howland, p. 143.)

She then describes how her technique as an actress works. 'You accept to let go, utterly and the power to be flows in and circulates like a healthy blood stream.' (p. 144) By turning away from herself she finds freedom behind the mask of the character. By turning to the Other in yourself through the mask, you find your creativity. In *Africa Slingshot* the mask is a trick – the hero in the play is a kind of Anancy. The powerful outsider is a charismatic leader but he cannot facilitate the promised change because he is not authentic. He is discredited when his past overwhelms him and the project falls apart.

Outside of the obvious lesson that we must be careful of strangers and charismatic storytellers, I want to read this story as a covert staging of the drama of racial crisis described by Fanon in *Black Skin White Masks* (1967). There, Fanon describes in a very famous passage, the crushing effects of the gaze of a white child at a black skinned Martinican. When the child calls out 'Look! A negro.' (p. 95) The mask of identity constructed around racist mythologies shatters and creates for the black subject a profound existential crisis. Fanon describes the phenomenon in relation to the colonized but it is also possible to infer from his discussion that the binaries of domination and subordination established in the drama of colonizer/colonized requires the colonizer to assume a mask of domination which can be shattered when challenged.

I read Howland's texts through Fanon's description of this crisis. It is a crisis that she is perhaps able to express for two reasons. First she is a white woman and therefore perhaps socialized to embrace an existential vulnerability. Second, as a performer and writer she is able to grasp the importance of the mask to social roles on stage and off. As Fanon proposes the drama of domination and difference can only be resolved when and if both parties agree to recognize each other and to reject their masks. For Fanon this happens through confrontation. For Howland this confrontation can begin to happen where performance works as a space for confronting the audience with its defences. For her this confrontation must take place for both the powerful and the powerless, if identity is to be remade. As the trickster's power slips away when he is confronted and his mask stripped off, so Howland's power as a writer slips away when the unresolved issues of her past overwhelm her. In the *The Long Run* she describes the difficult process of remaking her own identity in writing her autobiography after leaving Jamaica.

Lack of recognition and the crisis of inauthenticity are also enacted in *Return to Paradise* and *The Impossible Situation*, her plays about domestic workers. In both cases the racialized class conflict that structures society is between women of different classes in the domestic, not the public sphere. In *Return to Paradise*, Annie returns to her old employer and asks for recognition in the form of a job, but the middle-class woman responds through an assertion of her dominance. She literally closes the door and the dialogue ends. Jean, the daughter of the household is able to provide some vestige of hope by listening to Annie's story of her young Grandson's drift into crime. While she is not able to act, like the audience she is in some sense able to hear the voice of the Other as she speaks her pain before the gates to the urban garden and household are closed against her.

While *Return to Paradise* like *Impossible Situation* and *Uncle Robert* are set in middle-class homes, *The Creatures* is Howland's most adventurous attempt to represent African Jamaican culture, for while it owes much to the tradition of French mime it also attempts to translate to the stage the figure of River Mumma, Myamaid which roughly equates with Oshun in the Yoruba tradition and with Mami Wata in other African cultures. But it too is a tale of rejection, in which the young woman rejected by her beloved is reclaimed and comforted by the water goddess while the woman who remains in the world is embittered by the failure of romance. The play is an early attempt at staging cultural hybridity seriously. That is, the play attempts to stage an African presence seriously and not in the comic form that tended to be the norm at the time. The animal chorus and the central metaphor of the river are borrowed from the symbolism of the theatre of Dullin and St. Denis. Howland attempts to mix these with elements of African diasporic religion. Perhaps here stylistically the recognition and exchange that has to happen across difference begins covertly through the dramatic imagery.

It also begins when people came to together across class and colour to represent themselves in a formal cultural institution such as the theatre from which they had been excluded. This was the importance of the creative summer workshops at Knox College in which Howland collaborated with Errol Hill, playwright and

Extramural Tutor in Drama at the University of the West Indies. Through these initial efforts the theatre became a public space for limited social contact between the classes.

Class, taste, confrontation and dialogue

But precisely because of Howland's formation and training and the European tastes of the middle class, the dramaturgical language used for depicting Jamaican culture in *The Creatures* and the plays is the language of high art. This and other work written for the newly formed Extramural Dept of the University of the West Indies in the 1950s addressed middle-class audiences. We know this because the dramaturgical values themselves make this clear. Howland's work (with the possible exception of *Sleepy Valley*) was based on written text and drew on Aristotelian principles often borrowing Western classical elements such as the Chorus from Greek Drama. Like Una Marson in *Pocomania* and Frank Hill in *Upheaval*, her main legacy is as a writer of drama rather than popular comedy which got its impetus from working-class 'downtown' performances such as those of the UNIA and the Sunday morning variety concerts of Cupidon, Slim and Sam and others. Working with Errol Hill, the director and scholar who imagined Caribbean theatre combined high art, folk tradition and complex Black characters, she experimented with creating a hybrid theatre of empathy that presented 'West Indians', as figures of empathy and not comic stereotypes. Her work along with that of the Walcott brothers and, in the next decade Barry Reckord, moved the theatre away from offerings of comedy duos, satire, improvisation and variety shows that had characterized the popular offerings at Marcus Garvey's Edelweiss Park. It also moved it away from the light popular 'folk' musical such as the annual Pantomime of the Little Theatre Movement. Howland's formation in France helped her to approach the challenges of creating a theatre of empathy. One writer to the *Daily Gleaner* commenting on the success and failures of these attempts captured the efforts this way:

> At least it was about real Jamaican people in the setting of real Jamaican problems. At last the Jamaican labourer is permitted to be a serious dignified person on a Jamaican stage and colour and social change is faced as it should

be faced and handled as it should be handled – with the gloves off. *Daily Gleaner*, Monday March 3, 1943, p.6.

It was, as this writer shows, the middle class that needed to hear the social critique since they were the ones with the gloves on. An outsider who had not been fully formed by the colonial society but who came to it with the credentials of European cultural capital could perhaps begin to break through the hard shell of uneasy denial. Her stories urge her audience toward the self-reflexive, toward a renegotiation of values. They depend on what she describes as a awakening, brought about by a social movement that engendered self-awareness across classes. She describes the importance of the social movement – albeit in top down terms:

> Of course this awakening did not happen all by itself. It was sparked off and given direction, in the main by a group of left-wing intellectuals calling for self-government, and working hard towards that end against the odds of a die-hard colonial policy… (Howland, p. 107)

Conclusion

I asked at the start: what might Cicely Howland's plays have to offer us in terms of thinking about the practice of a radical multi-racialism in the Caribbean decades after they were written? I've suggested that such multi-racialism is only possible in the context of a social movement that creates a space for the making of meaning in the context of broader political, social and cultural ends. What Howland was able to say and not say in her writing, how she could say it and to whom – all this depended on how she negotiated two often contradictory factors: first, her own positioning as an outsider, a white elite Western-educated woman who was also an actress and writer, and second, her positioning within the liberal arm of the anti-colonial social movement in Jamaica, a movement committed to social progress through reform, multi-racial unity and cross-class alliance.

Howland, worked with a broad group of comrades who shared a particular cultural vision and a particular struggle against the 'bleak and narrow conventions' (p. 106) of their own class. With their support and later the support of Errol Hill's vision of an 'indigenous' theatre at the University, she wrote from within the complex network of conflicts that structured colonial society. As we see when we begin to decode Howland's symbols and narratives the theme of alienation, inauthenticity and rejection are key affects of social ideologies across the binaries of race. Once the mask of social roles begin to come down deep disorientation occurs on both sides. The crisis brought about by the challenge to the status quo is the opportunity to move beyond the fixity of identities and toward confronting new ways of being and doing in the society. At a time when the middle strata seems as concerned as ever with fixing the unruly, Howland's work reminds us that collective reflexivity is deeply generative. Confronting the vulnerabilities and social terrors of those who have a toehold on respectability is a precondition for the crossing of fixed borders to begin. Such crossings are never perfect or finite. But they are a beginning.

Honor Ford-Smith, Kingston, Jamaica
January 2012

References

Abraham, S. (2007) 'Multiculturalism as more than the sum of ethnicities', *Race and Class* October, Vol. 49 no. 2, 91-100.

Fanon, F. (1967) *Black Skin, White Masks.* New York: Grove Press.

Hill, E. (1992) *The Jamaican Stage 1655-1900.* Amherst: University of Massachusetts Press.

Howland, C. (1961) *The Long Run.* London: Victor Gollancz Ltd.

Waite-Smith, C. (1958) *Africa Sling Shot; a Play in One Act.* Mona, Jamaica, Extra Mural Department: University College of the West Indies.

Waite-Smith, C. (1966) *The Creatures.* Port-of-Spain, Trinidad & Tobago: University of the West Indies, Extra-Mural Department.

Waite-Smith, C. (1966) *The Impossible Situation.* Trinidad and Tobago: U.W.I., Extra Mural Department.

Waite-Smith, C. (1943) *Rains for the Plains and Other Stories.* Kingston, Jamaica: Printed by the Gleaner Co.

Waite-Smith, C. (1966) *Return to Paradise.* Trinidad and Tobago: U.W.I., Extra Mural Department.

Waite-Smith, C. (1957) *Uncle Robert (Family Poem) a Play in Three Acts.* Mona, Jamaica: Extra-Mural Department, University College of the West Indies, 1957.

Characters

RIVER

LIZARD

YELLOWLEGS

FISHERMAN (MAS ZEKIEL)

SAPHIRA

ROSE

CLEMMIE

MISS FANNY

MISS MAY

WINSTON

WILLIE

MAS CHARLIE

SEVERAL YOUNG MEN AND GIRLS
FROM THE VILLAGE

SCENE 1

A lonely spot by the river, a few chains from the village. Stage right, a rocky cliff rising from the reeds and tall grasses downstage extreme right to a fair height back centre right. A pathway winds up from L to R to a footbridge at the top. Only the end of the bridge and the rails are visible – the rest disappears off back R. This bridge spans the river which is invisible the other side of the rocky projection. Stage L a lovely shade tree.

It is evening, shortly before sundown – a lovely hour of peace by the river where the sun has at last lost its brutality and shines with the gentle golden splendour of decline.

LIZARD lies stretched on his back on the rock R. He is absolutely still. YELLOWLEGS, a tall heron-legged bird, dusky-backed, white-breasted with long black bill, stands among the reeds extreme R looking off downstream in a sort of trance. All is very quiet for a moment.

RIVER: *(Off. Calling in a clear, far-away pastoral voice.)* Fi-sher-maan…

LIZARD: *(Without moving.)* There's River calling the fisherman again.

YELLOWLEGS: *(Shifting slightly.)* He's late this evening.

LIZARD: Isn't it strange, Yellowlegs, I haven't heard her call anyone else like that for ages and ages.

YELLOWLEGS: Those three little boys who bathe naked downstream in the morning – you know, by the pool – she calls them.

LIZARD: I never heard her.

YELLOWLEGS: I do. She calls them ever so softly – like this *(Faint and high and fast.)* boy-boy-boy-boy-boy-boy. Usually just about the time the school bell rings.

LIZARD: *(Stretching and turning on his side.)* What do you think of that bell, by the way? It gets on my nerves – sends cold shivers up and down my spine.

YELLOWLEGS: Disturbing, yes. Even worse than the church bell. It breaks something every time.

LIZARD: It breaks time.

YELLOWLEGS: The rounded, continuous and perfect arc of heaven. That reminds me – it will soon be time for me to fly north. Have you heard the delicious mating songs? Spring is there, where the trees burst into leaf and a nest awaits on the shores of northern waters.

LIZARD: *(Dreamily.)* Water… You wouldn't think it, Yellowlegs, but I remember, in a dark part of me, the waters of warm pools and sluggish rivers washing a body like mine, but not mine, colossal, armoured, powerful!

YELLOWLEGS: Your ancestors.

LIZARD: Remote cousins of the blood, belly-crawling and terrible.

YELLOWLEGS: I remember one day as I stood feeding on a lonely bank, a rustle in the grass sent me springing to the nearest tree branch. There below was my enemy the snake who had crawled close to me in the grass. My heart trembled as I saw his unflickering eye of bead, his head lifted to watch me. Then I thought: I have looked into those eyes before: the eyes of my mate, the very same. Somewhere, how far away I can't remember, I too crawled on my belly through the grass – if there was grass. *(Spreading his wings.)* Yet surely the seeds of flight were in me already. Surely through obedience they have sprung up and have been glorified.

RIVER: *(As before.)* Fi-sher-maan…

LIZARD: She's getting impatient.

YELLOWLEGS: He'll soon be along now and sit there till dark staring down at her.

LIZARD: He doesn't really see her, does he?

YELLOWLEGS: You never know with humans. But I doubt it. *(Pause.)* Now she'd spinning. *(Long pause.)*

LIZARD: What's she doing now?

YELLOWLEGS: She's running the last gold threads off her loom.

RIVER: Fi-sher-maan…

YELLOWLEGS: He'd better hurry.

LIZARD: I think he's coming now.

> *The animals remain perfectly still as the FISHERMAN comes up from L. He's an ageless sort of man, not young but neither is he really old. A character. He wears hardworn trousers and shirt, is whistling or singing as he comes. He settles on rock elevation right with his legs dangling over into space and slowly baits and casts his line, whistling gaily all the while.*

FISHERMAN: *(As he casts his line.)* Evening, Yellowlegs. *(Y-L doesn't move.)* Oh go on with you, you know who I'm talking to. *(Y-L cocks his head slightly. FISHERMAN chuckles.)* Playing the woman with me, eh? All right, all right. *(Swinging suddenly round on his elbow.)* Lizard! I see your bright eye, watching me. How're things? *(He turns back to river, whistling. Pause.)* Mm. River's spinning again. Wonder if she's going to send up any of those darn, twisty little fish characters tonight? *(Tenderly.)* She's beautiful though, this woman of a river… Lady, you're running swift today. Rain up in the hills, eh? Ah you're a woman, a real woman, hiding, dancing, changing, sulking. *(He laughs.)* But a silent woman, eh, Yellowlegs? No? Well, anyway, not like the one up top there, scolding your life away. A beauty like this one, a real beauty. *(Long pause.)*

LIZARD: The sun drives his last stroke of love into my side. *(He stretches, sighs, slowly slides off his rock and makes a tour stage L, stretching and gazing up and about. He returns and stands leaning his elbow on rock, his head perched to attention, watching FISHERMAN after latter begins speaking again.)*

FISHERMAN: *(Over his shoulder.)* Stretching yourself, eh, after a gorgeous lazy day, eh Lizard? Not a stroke of work – your dinner just there tantalizing there under your very nose for you. Eh? Like a king… Strange and comforting how the creatures I care for never answer a word of protest or impertinence when I talk to them! Not like the old woman up there nagging a man's life away because he doesn't kill himself rushing round for jobs that probably don't even exist anyway. *(Imitating woman mockingly.)* 'Lord, how can you be so lazy! Look how I work and slave and wear myself out sewing and cleaning for a living to bring food to your pot and shelter to your worthless head!' *(Normally.)* Ah Miss Fanny! Well, that's her business. No one ever told her to wear herself out. Eh, Yellowlegs? *(Y-L is watching him too now, curiously.)* Wonder if you have woman trouble. No, I don't think so. I never see no ruffled female chasing you upstream with her claws in your tail. *(Suddenly jerking his line.)* Eheh! What's that? *(Relieved.)* False alarm, thank God. I didn't think you'd suddenly turn on me. You never yet send fish when I'm in a quiet peace-loving frame of mind. You understand me, don't you, River? Eh? *(Tenderly.)* Ah, you're sweet though.

It has been growing darker. YELLOWLEGS begins to flap his wings, getting ready for a move.

FISHERMAN: You going so soon? 'Men to their hearthstones and birds to their nests.' Goodnight. See you tomorrow! *(YELLOWLEGS wheels full circle round stage, wades out through reeds and disappears.)* Gone! *(Looking round.)* Lizard? You still here? *(Suddenly LIZARD springs away across stage to behind tree.)* Oops! What's biting him?

SAPHIRA appears at bridge head with a coal pot on her head and a lantern in her hand. She's a simple peasant girl in brief dress and bare feet.

FISHERMAN: Oh, it's you.

SAPHIRA: Mas Zekiel: you still here at this hour trailing that silly old line of yours in the river?

FISHERMAN: And you, Saphira Smith, what are you doing with that silly old coal pot on your head?

SAPHIRA: *(Depositing coal pot at foot of tree.)* Coal pot cooks dinner anyway. Mas Zeke, we're going to have a feast tonight.

FISHERMAN: A feast?

SAPHIRA: A big feast.

FISHERMAN: But not here? Not at this place?

SAPHIRA: Same place, right here.

FISHERMAN: Why you can't stay up in the village like sensible decent human beings?

SAPHIRA: Because we don't want to.

FISHERMAN: *(Concerned.)* Listen to me child. This is not a good place for a feast. If you must go gallivanting there's a much better place downstream a little – you know, under the guango tree, near Miss Elsie's yard. Now there's a place for a feast.

SAPHIRA: And have old Miss Elsie shushing us and preaching at us for having our fun? No Sir! Anyway, we like this place the best. Winston chose it himself.

FISHERMAN: *(Grumbling and putting up his rod.)* Why Winston have to go interfering. I want to know. He was always the interferingest child from he was born.

SAPHIRA: How you mean? The feast is for him himself. You don't remember he's off into the great wide world tomorrow morning?

FISHERMAN: True, true, I forgot.

SAPHIRA: Your own nephew. Shame!

FISHERMAN: Yes, the young eagle is spreading his wings. Though why he should want to go interfering with the wickedness of great cities and mighty continents I can't understand.

SAPHIRA: *(Tartly.)* At least he has a little ambition. That's more than anyone can say of you, Mas Zekiel.

FISHERMAN: *(Reproachfully.)* Hi Saphira, don't you go turn into that sort of a woman too. Keep your simplicity and your youth, my child. Don't go embittering up your sweet tongue with the heartlessness of hardened womanhood.

SAPHIRA: I'm sorry, Mas Zekiel. I didn't mean anything.

FISHERMAN: That's all right, that's all right. Child, come here. Hold up your lantern. There, over the water. *(They both kneel on the rock and lean over the river. Then, as though revealing a precious mystery.)* See her there? See her gliding like the dark snake of perdition? Slithering and contorting herself against the bank?

SAPHIRA: *(Fascinated for a moment.)* Yes…I remember once at my auntie's near the sea seeing the men fishing in the night with lights. The water looked just like that.

FISHERMAN: The sea is one thing. Everybody knows the sea is vast and foreign. But the river's different. People don't know. They say: 'Oh, the river, yes.' But they don't understand.

SAPHIRA: What they don't understand, Mas Zeke?

FISHERMAN: Her beauty, Saphira.

SAPHIRA: *(Gazes a moment, then laughs and moves away.)* Lord, Mas Zeke, what an imagination a man can have! Fancy you bewitched by that old river! And here I am listening to your great stories and I should be running back up to the village to help fetch down the food for the picnic.

FISHERMAN: Ah yes, the picnic. I forgot. Who and who are coming?

SAPHIRA: Most all the young people. Everybody loves Winston.

FISHERMAN: And you – you love Winston too?

SAPHIRA: Oh Winton never looks at me.

FISHERMAN: Foolish boy! You're the pearl of them all, Saphira.

SAPHIRA: Oh go away! Miss Fanny's coming too, to help.

FISHERMAN: *(Chuckling.)* Eh eh! Since when is she counting herself with the young? That's a good one.

SAPHIRA: She's your pearl, Mas Zeke.

FISHERMAN: *(Wincing.)* Oh don't mock me, Saphira. But I must get out of here quick before all this riotous youth arrives on me.

SAPHIRA: You mean before Miss Fan catches you!

He rises quickly and rips his trousers on a rock as he does so.

FISHERMAN: Lord my God, my trousers!

SAPHIRA: Mas Zeke! What Miss Fanny going to say to that now?

FISHERMAN: Are they badly torn?

SAPHIRA: *(Looking behind him, laughing and covering her mouth with her hands.)* Terrible! And in a most revealing place!

FISHERMAN: It's the devil's own work. Let me get out of here fast.

But it's too late. Two young girls, ROSE and CLEMMIE, come in laden with trays of food. ROSE is a bold, forward girl, CLEMMIE is an inveterate follower and giggler.

ROSE: There she is, Clemmie, sweetening up old Mas Zeke in the dark. *(CLEMMIE giggles.)*

SAPHIRA: Shame, Rose! Poor Mas Zeke!

ROSE: Mind now, Clemmie, don't laugh so much, you'll go dropping down your tray! *(She puts hers down under a tree.)* Come, Saphira, let us fix up the trays real nice.

Several older women and girls follow, carrying a large iron pot and more lanterns. Among these is MISS FANNY, MAS ZEKE's thorn in the flesh, a large and formidable woman; and MISS MAY, who is WINSTON's mother and MAS ZEKE's sister-in-law. They at once busy themselves lighting the coal pot. They are followed presently by a group of men, mostly young, among them WINSTON, carrying rum.

MISS FANNY: Come on, Miss May. Make us get the pot boiling quick time. This curry goat won't be no good if it's allowed to cool off.

MISS MAY: Right, Miss Fanny. My Winston's crazy about good hot curry goat. *(Seeing FISHERMAN who is standing with his back to the rock)* Eh oh, Miss Fanny, look who's here.

MISS FANNY: *(With terrible irony.)* Ah the fisherman, is it? What are you doing here, may I ask? I haven't seen you all day.

FISHERMAN: Nothing, Miss Fan. Nothing.

MISS FANNY: Nothing. That I can well believe, for you never yet done anything useful or that don't vex a woman to death.

FISHERMAN: *(Sliding upstage.)* I'm going right now, Miss Fan.

MISS FANNY: Wait a bit! What you walking sideway like a crab?

FISHERMAN: Was I walking sideways? I didn't notice.

MISS FANNY: You're hiding something. Turn round!

FISHERMAN: I wouldn't hide nothing from my own Miss Fan, you should know that.

MISS FANNY: Don't give me none of that talk. Turn round.

FISHERMAN: *(Suddenly vexed, bluffing.)* I'm not turning round. Why you always got to think the worst, eh? Suppose I had a surprise for you, what then? But no. You would always expect to find a serpent in the place of sweet-smelling roses.

MISS FANNY: *(Astonished.)* Zeke, what's come over you now?

FISHERMAN: *(Following his advantage.)* Now leave me, woman, while I go home in peace with the world.

MISS FANNY: *(With sudden inspiration and hope.)* Wait! I know! Don't tell me. You caught a fish! You're hiding it there, behind your back, to surprise me! You caught a fish at last, Zeke, and you know how I love a nice bit of fish cutlet and you have it there, hiding for me behind your back! Zeke! Turn round!

FISHERMAN: *(Warding her off.)* Now, now!

MISS FANNY: *(Swinging him vigorously round.)* Turn yourself, man, and show us.

> *Everybody sees the torn trousers. There is a burst of laughter. But MISS FANNY gazes with bitter anger and disappointment.*

MISS FANNY: *(Quieting everyone by her tone.)* A tear in his pants! That's all he has to offer me! A tear in his pants, God help me. *(Savagely.)* Fool that I was to think a worthless, good-for-nothing creature like you could ever bring anything but misery and disappointment to a woman. *(She begins to shake him hysterically.)* Come here, you feeble image of a man. I'm going to shake you till your teeth drop out! I'm going to shake you till your bones rattle! I've a good mind to murder you and have done with you! You – You –

MISS MAY: Miss Fan! Leave him alone now! He's not worth it. Don't take on so, you'll give yourself an attack!

MISS FANNY: *(Turning on her.)* And whose fault will that be? You're a fine one to talk when you've got good and rid of his brother these ten years and can live in peace and quiet without the burden of a worthless man!

SAPHIRA: It was an accident, Miss Fanny. He tore the pants on a rock, I saw him.

MISS FANNY: You shut your mouth and keep your eyes on your own business, Saphira Smith.

> *ROSE comes forward with some rum she taken from the men and poured into a mug.*

ROSE: Now, Miss Fanny, drink this up and you'll feel better. Come Miss Fanny.

MISS FANNY: *(Taking it.)* Lord me God, see my trial and my cross in this vale of tears and torments!

WINSTON: *(Offering bottle to FISHERMAN.)* You too, Uncle Zeke, take a drink now and forget your troubles and join us in the fun.

FISHERMAN: No, no, Winston my boy, I'll be going along now.

WINSTON: Come, Mas Zeke, just one pull.

FISHERMAN: Just one, then. A small one. *(He drinks deeply.)*

> *The boys with drum and banjo strike up the music. General reaction of pleasure. Some couples dance.*

ROSE: *(Who is dancing.)* Mas Zeke, come on, you must dance. I want to see Mas Zeke dance. Everybody! Who's got a pin to catch up Mas Zeke's pants?

YOUNG MAN: What's that about Mas Zeke's pant?

ROSE: *(Leaving her partner.)* A pin! I want a pin for Mas Zeke's pant!

MISS FANNY: *(Bustling forward from where she's been preparing food.)* Child! You think I can't look after my own man? Out of my way! *(Swinging ZEKE round and attacking pant.)* I carry needle and thread here in my bosom at all times.

A MAN: For all emergencies, eh Miss Fanny?

MISS FANNY: For all emergencies, you're right. Zeke, you worthless fisherman, stand still and let me fix you up.

> *He obeys humbly. Cries of 'Lord, Mas Zeke!… What a woman…' etc.*

WINSTON: *(Who has been dancing with one girl after another, not more than a few steps with each.)* Rose, gal, our turn now.

A MAN: You're dividing yourself up good and proper before you go, eh Winston?

WINSTON: Must, man.

ANOTHER MAN: Leaving a little bit of paradise for every girl to remember you by, eh?

WINSTON: Right!

MISS MAY: Fanny, you go watch the pot a while. I'm going to take a turn with Mas Zeke, now you've patched him up. Eh, Mas Zekiel?

FISHERMAN: Lord, Miss May, I don't dance nowadays. Pick one of the young ones, I'll tread your toes to pulp.

MISS MAY: Nonsense! Come on, man. My Jo's been gone a long time now. Come give me a bit of excitement, old man.

She draws him into dance and he whirls her round till they both stagger and everybody is laughing.

FISHERMAN: *(Panting.)* Well, there's your bit of excitement, Miss May.

MISS MAY: Lord me God, the man nearly killed me. My head's spinning round – my knees are giving way –

MISS FANNY: *(Dryly.)* Serve you right, Miss May. Come and take care of the food, good and respectable, where you belong.

MISS MAY: *(Joining her.)* I enjoyed it all the same.

YOUNG MAN: *(To CLEMMIE who stands by Banjo man.)* Clem, you not dancing tonight?

ROSE: *(Calling out.)* That's what happens to you, Clem, when you take up with a musician man like Willie. I warned you about it. *(CLEMMIE giggles.)*

YOUNG MAN: Come on, give us a dance.

CLEM: *(Shyly to WILLIE.)* Willie, you mind if I dance?

WILLIE: I don't mind if it's me you dance with. And, in fact, I'll dance with you myself. Out of my way, boy.

They dance. In consequence only the drum beats. Soon there are protests of: 'Lord, what is this?... Come, man, play your banjo... You can't leave off playing so?...' etc.

WILLIE: I'm dancing. I'm not playing. I'm dancing with my girl.

MISS FANNY: *(Above the noise.)* Food, friends! Food! The food is ready! Come one and all. Eat it while it's hot!

Drum stops. There is a great gathering round the food which is on the ground in the huge pot.

MISS MAY: Saphira, Clemmie – come pass round the plates.

MISS FANNY: Everybody walk up this way and get your curry goat. *(Cheers.)*

FISHERMAN: *(Right in it all now.)* Everybody walk up this way and get your rum. *(Louder cheers.)*

A MAN: To Winston, our brave pioneer. *(Cheers etc.)* Good luck to you, friend!

MISS MAY: I feel to break down and cry. My only son leaving me to go exploring distant lands all by himself, alone, without a friend by his side.

MISS FANNY: He'll do fine, your Winston, you wait and see.

SAPHIRA: There are friends, they say, wherever you go in the world. Miss May. He'll be all right.

MISS MAY: Winston, my boy!

MEN: Speech! Speech!

WINSTON: *(His mouth full of curry goat.)* Speech? Me?

EVERYBODY: Yes man… Come on, man… Speech!

WINSTON: *(Wiping mouth slowly with back of hand.)* Well…

A MAN: Here, let me hold your plate for you, man.

WINSTON: Well, friends…

ANOTHER MAN: Bravo! That's it, Winston, speak up.

WINSTON: Well – this is my village. *(He speaks slowly, searching for his thoughts and words.)* You're my friends. Yes, you're all my friends. *(Sounds of approval.)* And I'm going away. To the great city of Kingston. And then, God willing, to America. If there was decent jobs and all here – well – that would be different. Then I wouldn't go and leave all my friends and my village.

SEVERAL: That's right! You wouldn't have to…

WINSTON: But – well I guess there's lots of men in lots of villages going away to try and better themselves and add to their self-respect and see the world and give themselves a chance. So I'm going too. *(Pause.)* Well that's all.

ALL: Bravo, bravo, Winston, man.

SAPHIRA: *(Gazing at him with passionate admiration.)* That was a great speech. Winston.

SEVERAL: Yes, boy. You can really talk. What you say makes sense. It's the truth.

FISHERMAN: Come on. Fill up your glasses, everyone. Music, boys, music!

There is a buzz around the pot and the rum for a moment. The musicians are now seated and play softer and slower than before. Everyone begins eating and drinking in earnest. There's a little flirting, some indistinct conversation, an occasional high-pitched laugh from someone getting merry, some giggling from CLEMMIE. One or two couples get up and dance. The actors will supply this ad lib as they get into their parts. WINSTON has silently taken SAPHIRA's plate and put it on the ground and begun to dance with her. They move gradually into the shadows right. They stop dancing and he kisses her. Then they stand embraced looking into each other's eyes.

A MAN: Pep up the music there, boys. Rose and me want to dance.

ANOTHER: Willie and Sam here need a drink, eh Willie? Mas Zeke, pour drinks for these parched labouring boys.

ROSE: Quick time, Willie. We gotta dance now and shake down all the feed we've been having.

MISS FANNY: Mind you get yourselves one big indigestion.

MISS MAY: They're young, Miss Fanny, they're young. They don't know the meaning of indigestion. Now where's that Winston gone to? He's hardly eat.

A MAN: *(Calling.)* Winston! Come now, man. Spread yourself out a little now. Your mother's calling you. *(Louder.)* Winston!

WINSTON leaves SAPHIRA and joins group.

MISS MAY: Here, son, here's a nice hot dish of curry goat and banana for you. You've hardly eat.

WINSTON leans against tree and begins to eat. He and SAPHIRA are still looking at each other, from a distance now. The musicians have had a quick one.

MAN: Ready now boys?

SAM: Ready! We going really give you something now, eh Willie?

WILLIE: Right! Hot it up good for you, Clemmie, hold me glass till I'm through.

CLEMMIE: *(Admiringly.)* Yes, Willie darling.

Musicians go to town. ROSE and her man, take the floor with several other couples. They're all a bit high but not unsteady. There is a feeling of real vigour and gaiety. Suddenly SAPHIRA leans forward and takes FISHERMAN by the hands and pulls him down centre.

SAPHIRA: *(Bursting with joy and love.)* Mas Zeke, come dance with me! You must dance with me, you hear? I want to leap and sing and celebrate and rejoice! Come rejoice with me, Mas Zeke!

FISHERMAN: Right, right. Come then, gal. *(They dance and leap and whirl round and round as she cries.)*

SAPHIRA: I'm happy! Happy! Happy! I never been so happy never. Lord, Mas Zeke, in the whole world there was never anybody happy like me! Whirl me round fast fast!

FISHERMAN: Oops! Fly high, gal, fly high!

SAPHIRA: Faster, faster, faster… *(He responds to her spirit and they dance and turn wildly, ecstatically, as the curtain falls.)*

SCENE 2

Same as Scene One. Very early next morning. YELLOWLEGS is discovered alone. He is standing on the FISHERMAN's rocky ledge in a listening, attentive attitude. LIZARD comes in left.

LIZARD: Good morning Yellowlegs. A glorious lifting over there across the river. *(YELLOWLEGS does not appear to hear.)* What's the matter? Not well this morning? Not that

I'd blame you, after the deal of unnatural noise and fury waged here last night. Men are at war within themselves and the results are either frightening or ludicrous. *(Still YELLOWLEGS pays no attention.)* Friend, what is it? *(YELLOWLEGS slowly turns his head and looks at LIZARD. Pause, alarmed.)* Yellowlegs!

YELLOWLEGS: *(Shaking off his trance.)* You spoke to me?

LIZARD: You didn't hear me?

YELLOWLEGS: I think I heard your voice. But not what you said I was listening elsewhere. *(He suddenly stretches and flaps, trying his wings.)* The time for me is as near as the morning.

LIZARD: Oh. You'll be going soon then? Is that it?

YELLOWLEGS: This morning, while it was still dark, I thought I heard the golden hour of departure begin to sound its mighty voice. Calling. Calling to me.

LIZARD: I know how it is. Suddenly you just won't be here any longer. Then one day, soon after, the yellow-billed cuckoo, summering from South America, will arrive and walk your riverbank, nest in your tree. You'll see signs of him in the Fall you return.

YELLOWLEGS: Yes. He has already spoken to me through a hundred signs. His footprints have remained for me on reed and branch; his very wingprint has left a sign in the air for me. *(He cocks his head.)*

LIZARD: What are you listening to now? *(YELLOWLEGS doesn't reply.)* And I remain. *(With deep appreciation.)* It is good to remain in the same sun – always. *(Pause.)* Pst! Hear that? Never has any but the Fisherman intruded here at this hour. It's intolerable! *(He runs off right and YELLOWLEGS goes off left. We hear the girls off for a moment then they appear cautiously at the bridge-head.)*

CLEMMIE: What was that? I heard a noise.

SAPHIRA: *(Anxiously.)* You don't think he's gone already?

ROSE: No. of course he's not gone. The bus doesn't leave till seven.

SAPHIRA: Suppose they went down early?

CLEMMIE: What a fretful child! When I left home Miss May had just come out into the yard to catch the fire.

ROSE: He's probably still snoring, your Winston.

CLEMMIE: *(Excitedly.)* Saphira, what are you going to say when he comes? Lord, Saphira, the way he kissed you and stood and looked at you last night! What are you going to say?

SAPHIRA: *(Seating herself at the foot of tree; with simple faith.)* I don't know. But when he sees me, he'll come and speak to me and then I'll tell him goodbye –

CLEMMIE: And then he'll kiss you!

SAPHIRA: *(Anxious.)* D'you think so Clemmie?

ROSE: After last night! Of course!

CLEMMIE: What will you say then?

ROSE: What you think, foolish? *(Acting it out.)* That she loves him, and 'Please to take me with you!' and 'You can't leave me here now all alone,' and 'Winston my love' and 'Winston my darling.' *(CLEMMIE is giggling madly: ROSE embraces her.)* 'Oh Winston, I can't live without you.'

CLEMMIE: *(Laughing wildly.)* And what'll he say then?

ROSE: He'll try and kiss her, like this, but she won't let him right away and she'll run – Run, Clemmie! – But he'll catch hold of her, like this, but you must resist mind, Saphira. Oh, Clemmie, you're no good, any man could have you any time, for the asking!

SAPHIRA: *(Blushing and laughing.)* Shush Rose, you're too terrible! Why do you tease me so? Suppose he hears you!

ROSE: *(Serious.)* All right. You tell us. We won't laugh. Tell us what you'll say.

CLEMMIE: Yes, do. *(They sit down by her.)*

SAPHIRA: I tell you I don't know what I'll say. But I know the the Lord will help and put the right words in my mouth. *(Slowly and shyly.)* I know what I feel. I know I love him like I've never loved anybody, even my mother. Maybe he thinks I just wanted a good time last night, though; maybe he doesn't know I love him. But I shan't be afraid to tell him.

CLEMMIE: *(Moved.)* I think he knows it. I'd know it. Your face was all different, like the sun. Probably he's even changed his mind and won't be going away at all.

SAPHIRA: *(Quietly.)* I don't mind. As long as he'll let me wait for him. They don't keep them in America more than six months, Mas Zeke says. That's nothing.

ROSE: Suppose he goes and settles in Kingston?

SAPHIRA: I'm not afraid of Kingston. I don't mind where we are so long as I can do for him. *(LIZARD has come out from behind tree and watches them.)*

CLEMMIE: I think it's beautiful. Maybe Willie and me could go to Kingston too. What you think, Rose?

ROSE: I'd go to Kingston, sure…but I don't ever want to put all my money on one man. Not for Kingston or even for America. Not me.

SAPHIRA: *(Jumping up suddenly.)* Is that them? I heard something.

CLEMMIE: *(Who has run up to bridge head as LIZARD vanishes.)* Not yet. But I can see people gathering near the shop. *(Returning.)* Suppose lots of people go down to the bus with him, Saphira?

ROSE: It doesn't matter. He's bound to stop and say goodbye to her.

CLEMMIE: *(Hopefully.)* You want us to stay with you?

ROSE: Of course she doesn't, foolish!

CLEMMIE: You know what, Saphira? You'll go and stay in Kingston a while, and then when Winston has saved enough money you'll both come back and get married in the church here!

SAPHIRA: Stop, Clemmie. You're too foolish!

CLEMMIE: Miss Fan will make you a lovely white dress, you only have to send her the cloth, and maybe a picture of the style, and –

SAPHIRA: Shush, Clem, do shush! Those are dreams.

CLEMMIE: Dreams can come true. Everybody knows that. Winston's dream of America's coming true, isn't it?

ROSE: *(Who is watching at bridge head.)* Hi! They're coming.

SAPHIRA: Oh Clemmie!

CLEMMIE: *(Embracing her.)* I wish you happiness, Saphira.

ROSE: *(Coming down quickly.)* Here they come, Quick!

CLEMMIE: *(Scared suddenly.)* Let's go then.

SAPHIRA: No, please! Don't leave me.

ROSE: Don't be a silly. Come on, Clem.

> *They exit left. Voices are heard. In a panic SAPHIRA crouches down right behind a rock. WINSTON, dressed in a new shirt and pants and stiff new shoes, enters. With him are MISS MAY, MISS FANNY and a group of six or seven friends, including MAS CHARLIE, an old farmer. One of the men carries WINSTON's brand new cardboard suitcase. They are in that boisterous send-off mood that infects friends at the happy departure of a local hero.*

FIRST MAN: Brother, when you've walked the highways of the world a while we'll not know you, you'll be that grand.

SECOND MAN: You mustn't go forgetting your old pals, you know, boy.

WINSTON: Not likely! I'll be expecting you all to visit me in Kingston soon as I get back from America and settle down.

FIRST MAN: If you don't go and stay in America.

THIRD MAN: He'll come back. What a way we'll show those Kingston folk how country boys can jig and jive, eh?

FOURTH MAN: And drink up their liquor!

FIRST MAN: Right!

There is a good deal of laughing and backslapping during above.

SECOND MAN: Lord, sir! You seen Winston's smart sports shirt? The latest thing!

MAS CHARLIE: You not going to look like no country boy, son. You're real smart.

WINSTON: They say it's best not to let on you're from the country.

MAS CHARLIE: Yes sir! They say the thieves is something terrible in our capital city.

THIRD MAN: They say they'll murder you for your money without batting an eyelid.

MISS MAY: Lord me God! Careful, son, you hear. Careful!

WINSTON: I know how to take care of myself, Mama

FOURTH MAN: Sure, Miss May. Winston knows how to take care of himself. You can't fool our Winston.

MISS MAY: *(Annoyed.)* You can talk, young man. You too foolish yourself! Mas Charlie, what time is it now?

WINSTON: What you worrying about, Mama?

MISS FANNY: From now on, Winston, you got to watch the time, what with travelling on buses and trains and maybe even aeroplanes.

MISS MAY: Don't talk about it, Miss Fan. It makes my heart turn over in my bosom.

MAS CHARLIE: *(Who has solemnly taken out a huge old timepiece, the only watch in the village.)* The correct time is sixteen minutes past six o'clock.

MISS FANNY: Lots of time, Miss May.

FIRST MAN: Wait till Winston comes back – he'll have a fine American watch with one of those broad gold bands. Won't you, Winston?

WINSTON: Sure thing.

MISS FANNY: Winston, you sure you haven't forgotten anything? You have your sandwiches?

MISS MAY: *(Irritably.)* How would he forget anything when it's me myself who put in each and every one of his things with my own hands?

MISS FANNY: If it's you that put the things in, in your state of confusion and misery, God help the boy! He'll go naked in the streets of Kingston!

MISS MAY: *(Hotly.)* You know nothing of a mother's love, Miss Fan, or you'd never talk so foolish!

MISS FANNY: *(Fiercely.)* Is that so indeed? Just because I don't have no children of my own –

MAS CHARLIE: Ladies, is this the time for quarrelling, when our native son is about to set out on his great journey?

MISS MAY: Pcha!

THIRD MAN: Winston, you must find someone to write for you and send and tell us all about the girls up there. Eh, man?

MISS MAY: Winston son, you must send a letter soon soon, you hear? Tell us how you find Aunt Annie and what sort of work you get and how you're keeping and if they're going to send you to America. Won't you my boy?

WINSTON: Yes, Mama. I promised you already. I'll give you all the news.

They have now slowly but surely crossed the stage and are about to go off left.

SAPHIRA: *(Moving forward shyly. He turns to her, hesitating.)* Winston, I'd like to say goodbye to you.

WINSTON: *(Calling after others who go off.)* Go on, I'll join you in a minute. *(He returns to her. They look at each other awkwardly.)*

WINSTON: Well – goodbye, Saphira.

SAPHIRA: So you're off to Kingston, Winston.

WINSTON: That's right.

SAPHIRA: And maybe to America even.

WINSTON: That's right.

SAPHIRA: That's wonderful. I know you'll do well for yourself, Winston.

WINSTON: I hope so, Saphira.

SAPHIRA: What you plan to do exactly, Winston? I mean – you must have a sort of idea in your head. An ambition.

WINSTON: Well – I want to better myself. Make a little money to start myself up in a little business of something in the city.

SAPHIRA: *(Encouragingly.)* I know one boy saved enough money in America to start himself up as a tailor.

WINSTON: Yes, I heard so. And Nathaniel Rogers is a carpenter now in Kingston.

SAPHIRA: *(Pause, shyly.)* You'll need a good woman with you. Won't you?

WINSTON: Oh I'm not thinking of a steady woman right now.

SAPHIRA: Oh I know. I don't mean now. But when you come back from America.

WINSTON: That's looking too far ahead, Saphira.

SAPHIRA: *(Very low, ashamed.)* Not for me, it isn't. Winston can I wait for you? I mean wait till you come back and then –

WINSTON: But Saphira –

SAPHIRA: Will you send for me when you get back? I don't care how long I wait.

WINSTON: *(Weakly.)* Look Saphira, I can't ask any girl to wait for me.

SAPHIRA: But I want to. *(Going near.)* You know what, Winston? I always think it's you and me they mean in all those songs from America on the radio at the shop. You and me.

WINSTON: Look Saphira, I'm not figuring to fool you. I'm not getting tied up with any woman now.

SAPHIRA: Last night, Winston, you said I was your girl?

WINSTON: *(Frightened by her persistence.)* That was a dance, Saphira. You can't hold a man to every little thing he says at a dance. You're a nice girl.

SAPHIRA: *(Going closer to him.)* Why won't you let me be your girl and wait for you? That's not much to ask, is it?

WINSTON: Then you wait for me and I don't come back or I get another girl and then there's hell to pay. I know women.

SAPHIRA: *(Grasping his arms.)* Winston! Look at me like you did last night!

WINSTON: *(Throwing her aside so that she backs against the rock.)* Let me go. I'm not having no girl clinging onto me now, see? And when I do, it will be a town girl with some education and not any country girl. *(SAPHIRA looks at him with stricken eyes.)* Well, you asked for it. There's no use fooling you, is there?

MISS MAY: *(Off.)* Win-ston!

MAN: *(Off.)* Winston, come on, boy!

WINSTON: *(Calling.)* Coming! *(He looks at SAPHIRA, hesitates, then goes off quickly.)*

SAPHIRA is alone. She starts to cry in a strange, silent way, her whole body shaking as she leans against the rock. A time, then behind her RIVER appears, head and shoulders above the rocks. She is a handsome and seductive woman, wearing a dark greenish gown. She looks down at SAPHIRA.

RIVER: Listen, Saphira. I will take away all your tears and all your pain. Stretch out your hand to me and I will give you peace. Come. *(She holds out her hand.)*

SAPHIRA: *(Suddenly afraid.)* No, no! Mas Zekiel said you were the dark snake of perdition.

RIVER: *(Smiling.)* Do you know what perdition means?

SAPHIRA: No.

RIVER: It means to be lost.

SAPHIRA: Are you lost?

RIVER: No, Saphira. You're lost. I'm here to show you the way home. The way back.

SAPHIRA: *(Crying again.)* I don't want to go home. I don't want to go back.

RIVER: Tell me what you want.

SAPHIRA: Nothing – now. He's gone away and he doesn't love me.

RIVER: Tell me what you want.

SAPHIRA: I don't know. Nothing.

RIVER: *(More and more persuasively.)* Tell me what you want.

SAPHIRA: I – *(She breaks down.)*

RIVER: Tell me.

SAPHIRA: I want to die.

RIVER: *(Nodding.)* Yes.

SAPHIRA: *(Frightened.)* What d'you mean?

> *FISHERMAN comes in left with rod and pan. Stands in horror watching SAPHIRA.*

RIVER: Death comes to everyone, but few are wise enough to choose death at the right moment. It is a great privilege to have death come at the very time he is called on. You are privileged, Saphira.

SAPHIRA: *(Dully.)* I don't understand.

RIVER: My waters are deep and swift. There will be no trouble. No ugliness. No pain. It will be over quickly, and all you will know is the warmth of my arms and the singing of my voice in your ears.

FISHERMAN: *(In a low choked voice.)* No.

SAPHIRA: *(Echoing his cry but unaware of his presence.)* No. I'm afraid to die.

RIVER: I know. You want love, not death.

SAPHIRA: *(Moving nearer river.)* Yes.

RIVER: Death is an ugly word. You want love. But not Winston's love. That hurts too much. Didn't it hurt?

SAPHIRA: It was wonderful. He kissed me. He held me in his arms.

RIVER: But didn't it hurt today, when he left?

SAPHIRA: *(Crying softly.)* Oh yes.

RIVER: I will give you a love that doesn't hurt at all. Come to me.

FISHERMAN: No Saphira!

SAPHIRA: No I'm afraid.

RIVER: This morning he said he didn't want you.

SAPHIRA: *(Breaking down.)* I know.

RIVER: He said he'd have another girl.

> *SAPHIRA sobs wildly.*

RIVER: *(Relentlessly.)* This morning he threw you aside.

SAPHIRA: Oh God.

RIVER: He said he would never love an ignorant country girl like you.

SAPHIRA: Oh dear Jesus…

RIVER: *(Urgently.)* Come Saphira. Come to me. Come.

> *SAPHIRA, sobbing violently, throws herself into RIVER's arms. RIVER clasps her tight and bears her slowly away.*

FISHERMAN: *(Suddenly finding his voice and his senses.)* No, no, don't Saphira! Oh my God, come back, child! Where are you? Where are you? *(He has reached the bank and desperately scans the RIVER.)* Oh my God, what have you done to her! Saphira! *(Shouting.)* SAPHIRA!

All is quiet. He stares vacantly at the RIVER.

She's gone. I tried. I called out to her. I did all I could. She wouldn't hear. She just – didn't hear me.

Low voices are heard off left. WINSTON and all his send-off party return. It's a very deflated group compared with their earlier exuberance. WINSTON is carrying his own suitcase now. He sets it down and mops his brow. All stop.

WINSTON: *(Seeing FISHERMAN who has slowly turned to stare at them.)* It broke down. The bus broke down.

MISS MAY: Winston, I tell you it's an omen.

WINSTON: *(Wearily.)* What foolishness, Mama. Machines will break down sometimes.

MISS MAY: Foolishness eh? Same thing happened once to your aunt. But she heeded the warning. And when the bus finally left, what you think happened?

WINSTON: *(Impatiently.)* We all know that story.

MISS MAY: The bus turned over onto a gully and three people were killed, that's what happened.

FIRST MAN: Anyway Winston, old boy, they'll send to Kingston for a mechanic or there'll be another bus on Thursday. You'll be all right.

WINSTON: Sure.

ROSE: *(Pointedly.)* Maybe there'll be one or two that'll be glad the bus broke down. Eh, Clemmie?

CLEMMIE: Yes, Winston.

MAS CHARLIE: Well, it's getting late. And to think I fixed myself up in my best clothes all for nothing! *(He has drawn out his huge watch.)* Better get back to the field. Eh boys?

SEVERAL: Sun's high… Can't afford to idle all day… Come on, let's get going… OK Winston…

They follow MAS CHARLIE off right by bridge.

MISS FANNY: Come on, Miss May. Don't fret. You can't talk sense into a boy's head. You can only pray that God in His eternal mercy will hear, and hearing see, and seeing act.

MISS MAY: *(Sighing deeply.)* Ah my child! God in his wisdom sees and knows all, even into dark corners of a mother's heart. Come, Winston.

WINSTON picks up his suitcase.

MISS FANNY: *(Sharply.)* And you, Mas Zekiel, my fine fisherman, don't you go wasting any more time down here by the river. I've got things for you to do. Come on now.

FISHERMAN: *(Without moving.)* Yes, I soon come.

MISS FANNY: Come, Miss May. *(They start off. WINSTON pauses.)*

WINSTON: *(Forlorn.)* You see Saphira anywhere, Mas Zeke?

FISHERMAN: Saphira? *(He pauses. Shakes his head.)*

WINSTON: Thought you might have seen her. *(He starts off.)* OK Mas Zeke. *(He exits, despondent at the anti-climax of his departure. FISHERMAN sits down slowly, his legs weak, and stares blankly at the RIVER. LIZARD comes on from behind tree. He watches FISHERMAN a moment.)*

LIZARD: *(Calling.)* Yellowlegs! *(Waits.)* Ah, here he comes. *(YELLOWLEGS enters.)* I thought perhaps you'd gone. Did you hear what went on here a while ago?

YELLOWLEGS: No. But I saw something.

LIZARD: What?

YELLOWLEGS: Her body in the river.

LIZARD: Ah.

YELLOWLEGS: Was it terrible?

LIZARD: On the whole, no. There was a moment of horrible pain when she struggled with herself – that was terrible, as it always is. I wish they wouldn't live like that. He's doing it now too. *(Indicating FISHERMAN.)* There'll be no peace around here any more.

YELLOWLEGS: Then what happened?

LIZARD: Then she decided, and surrendered herself, and all went off quite naturally after that.

YELLOWLEGS: All the same, this riverbank is becoming much too popular – parties, love affairs, departures, suicides…

LIZARD: Perhaps after this they'll come less often.

YELLOWLEGS: He's all right. But the others…

LIZARD: Not today, he isn't. Look at him.

YELLOWLEGS: I've been looking at him. He's at war. He's forgotten us. *(Suddenly.)* Careful! Someone's coming! *(They go out left and right quickly.)*

ROSE: *(Off.)* Mas Zeke! Mas Zek-iel!

ROSE and CLEMMIE run on over bridge but remain at top of path for this scene.

CLEMMIE: Mas Zeke, Miss Fan says you must come now.

ROSE: She says she's not waiting more than five minutes.

FISHERMAN: *(Dully.)* All right. I'm coming.

CLEMMIE: She's in a rage about something.

ROSE: As usual. Five minutes, mind.

FISHERMAN: I'll be there.

ROSE: You'd better come quick then. *(Teasing.)* No fishing for you today, Mas Zeke. *(Coming down a bit.)* Tell me something truly. Have you ever caught a fish? *(He doesn't answer.)* Shame! I thought as much.

CLEMMIE: *(Giggling.)* Maybe it's a girl he comes down to meet here first thing in the morning and last thing in the evening.

FISHERMAN: Go away, both of you.

ROSE: All right then. But we're going to tell Miss Fan, you hear?

CLEMMIE: But if you tell us your secret we'll say nothing. We promise.

FISHERMAN: Stop bothering me.

ROSE: As you please. But Miss Fan will be bothering you with the lash of her tongue and maybe the lash of your own leather belt if you don't get a move on!

FISHERMAN: *(Rising, terrible, the tide of a lifetime breaking loose.)* Go away, go away, you women! Out of my sight! I'm tired of your jabbering mouths and you narrow hearts! My whole life has been dominated by women! From now on I'm going to be free. You hear? Free from you all! *(Menacing them.)* Go on, run now, run!! *(Suddenly, as they turn to go in alarm.)* Wait! I'm going to give you a fine story to tell up in the village – a story that will keep your mouths busy for a month! Saphira's dead. She leapt in to the river, there, and drowned. *(They gaze in horror towards the river.)* Oh, she's gone – gone to the sea now. You'll not see her again. Not get a chance to turn her into a sour woman prattling in her doorway and turning a man's life in on him. She's gone young and clean to the sea. Run now! Run and tell your story! *(Shouting.)* Go on! Run or I'll give you such a hiding you'll never forget it. Be gone!

They scamper away like terrified mice.

FISHERMAN: *(With a new burst of aggression.)* You too, River – Mrs River – woman – you too, you're the same as the rest. Treacherous, nagging and selfish as hell itself. *(He is trembling now and he sits down. A long pause while LIZARD quietly creeps back and watches him.)* All right, all right. I didn't mean it. I won't leave you. But what did you do to that poor girl! Poor gentle Saphira. Poor child. *(Pauses,*

a sigh.) I suppose Lizard is laughing at me for making a
woman out of you. A woman out of a blooming river.
(Defiantly.) Just – water. That's what you are. *(He throws
a stone in.)* See? I'm free. You're just – water. *(Suddenly
coaxing.)* No, no, don't be angry. I didn't mean it. I tell
you I didn't mean it. Come on, smile for me again, mm?
Woman… Lovely woman… *(Turning to LIZARD.)* My
friend. Restore peace and order here again. *(Noticing
YELLOWLEGS' absence.)* Where's Yellowlegs got to?

*They suddenly both lift their heads and follow with their eyes a
flight across the sky.*

FISHERMAN: *(With awe.)* Gone. Serene and free. No visible
force can ever dictate his going or his comings. Gone.
His flight guided by the wonder of the world. *(Pause.
LIZARD stretches himself and takes up same position on rock as
at beginning of play. FISHERMAN looks around him with a bit
of the old twinkle in his eye.)* You and I alone, eh Lizard?

RIVER: *(Calling, as at beginning of play.)* Fi-sher-man…

FISHERMAN: Hear that? She's jealous. Thinks I've forgotten
her. Coming, coming. *(He turns to RIVER and begins baiting
his line. Then he starts singing softly.)*

Curtain falls.

Ellen Cairns

Ellen Cairns trained at Glasgow School of Art and the Slade. She received the Arts Council Bursary in 1981 and subsequently became resident designer at Liverpool Playhouse during the Artistic Directorship of Chris Bond, Willy Russell, Alan Bleasdale and Bill Morrison. She became a freelance designer in 1989 during which time has designed over 50 productions notably *Moon on a Rainbow Shawl* (Almeida), *Fences* (Garrick Theatre), *Amen Corner* (Bristol Old Vic), *Blood Brothers* (Tel Aviv), *Carmen* (Sweden), *Dragon Can't Dance* (Stratford East), *Elvira Madigan* (Sweden), *Gods Are Not To Blame* (Riverside Studios), *Into The Woods* (Sweden), *Jubilee* (Stockholm), *King Lear* and *Resurrections* (Cochrane Theatre), *Poppy* and *Moll Flanders* (Half Moon), *Nicholas Nickleby* and *Angels in America* (Estonia), *Othello* (Drill Hall), *Porgy and Bess* (Venice), *Sweeney Todd* (Theatre Clwyd) *Trafford Tanzi* (Mermaid Theatre), *Fiddler on the Roof* and *Nicholas Nickleby* (Stockholm), *A Little Shop of Horrors* (Estonia). She has been associated with the award winning Talawa Theatre Company where she designed several productions and her designs for *King Lear* are are now part of the Victoria and Albert Theatre Archive. She is a visiting tutor in Theatre Design at Central Saint Martins College.

Honor Ford-Smith

Poet, playwright, author, actor and academic, was born in Montreal Canada in the Fifties. When she was three months old, her Jamaican mother took her home where she was raised among women in a middle-class, intergenerational household eventually enrolling at the University of the West Indies, before studying drama in the United States and Canada. She subsequently taught for several years at the Jamaica School of Drama. In 1977, she became a co-founder of Sistren Theatre, a Collective of mainly working-class women that represented images of women in theatre and built awareness around questions of gender and class through drama in education. In 1991, Ford-Smith enrolled with the Ontario Institute for Studies in Education University of Toronto, where she earned a Ph.D. for her thesis: 'Performing Nation, the pedagogy and politics of post-colonial Jamaican performance'. Her first book of poetry, *My Mother's Last Dance* was published in 1996. In 2005, *Just Jazz* her adaptation of Jean Rhys' 'Let Them Call It Jazz' was staged in Toronto. In 2011 she edited and wrote the scholarly introduction to *Three Jamaican Plays*, published by Paul Issa Press. She currently teaches in the Faculty of Environmental Sciences at York University.

Noel Dexter

Noel Dexter OD, graduated from the University of the West Indies with a degree in Sociology in 1967. His scholarship in Ethnomusicology, Jamaican Folklore and his distinguished career in teaching are well documented but it is his remarkable gift for musical direction in the theatre and most especially with choirs which has made him a household name in Jamaica.

In 1962 he founded the legendary Kingston Singers and was its Musical Director for twenty five years during which time the choir performed extensively in Jamaica and overseas to great acclaim. In 1974 his award winning Ardenne High School choir represented Jamaica at the Caribbean Festival of Arts (CARIFESTA) in Cuba. In 1977 he was appointed Director of Music at the Mona Campus of the University of the West Indies which post he held until his retirement in 2002. Under his musical direction the University Singers achieved critical acclaim not only in the Caribbean but internationally performing for heads of state and royalty and continue to enjoy the benefits of his inspired on-going musical direction.

Among his many awards are the Jamaican national honour of the Order of Distinction for his services in the field of music, The Institute of Jamaica Silver Musgrave Medal and the Prime Minister's Medal.

Yvonne Brewster

Jamaican born Yvonne Brewster OBE studied Drama at Rose Bruford College in London. She founded two theatre companies, the **Barn** in Jamaica and **Talawa** in England. She has worked in film, television, radio, and universities nationally and internationally as director, lecturer and actor. She is a Fellow of Rose Bruford College, the Central School of Speech and Drama, and the Royal Society of Arts, and is a Licentiate of the Royal Academy of Music. In 1993 she received the OBE for Services to the Arts and in 2001 an Honorary Doctorate from the Open University and the National Black Theatre Festival Living Legend Award (USA). She is editor of three collections in the Methuen series *Black Plays* and *For The Reckord,* a collection of plays by Barry Reckord published by Oberon Books in 2010. Her autobiography *The Undertaker's Daughter* was published in 2004.

Acknowledgements:

I am most grateful to Professor Mervyn Morris, Professor Sandra Richards, Deirdre van Outersterp, Lara Howland, Dr. Hazel Bennett, Jackie Guy, Buddy Pouyatt and Starr Brewster for their help in the long process of dusting off the past.

Yvonne Brewster